COLBY JUNIOR
COLLEGE
TOWN OF NEW LONDON
1779
NEW HAMPSHIRE
COLBY JUNIOR COLLEGE FOR WOMEN
PARATAE SERVIRE
MENS ANIMUS
CORPUS
1837
FRIENDS
OF THE
LIBRARY

Catullus in English Poetry

A complete index of poems, arranged as a Table of Contents, has been specially prepared for this edition and will be found at the back of the book.

Catullus in English Poetry

BY

ELEANOR SHIPLEY DUCKETT, Ph.D., D. Lit.
Associate Professor of Latin, Smith College

NEW YORK / RUSSELL & RUSSELL

Smith College Classical Studies
Number 6

FIRST PUBLISHED IN 1925
REISSUED, 1972, BY RUSSELL & RUSSELL
A DIVISION OF ATHENEUM PUBLISHERS, INC.
L. C. CATALOG CARD NO: 76-173518
PRINTED IN THE UNITED STATES OF AMERICA

PREFACE

With the effort of the present day to humanize the humanities the fashion has developed of issuing books which may set forth and sum up for the general reader the civilization of the peoples of ancient Greece and Rome. Translations of their works are provided in the *Loeb Library*, expositions and explanations of their life and thought are afforded in such books as *The Pageant of Greece*, *The Legacy of Greece*, *The Legacy of Rome*, or in those of the English series, *The Library of Greek Thought*, and of the larger American series, *Our Debt to Greece and Rome*, which also trace the influence of individual authors on later literature. In a short while all the fields of ancient thought and literature which are likely to prove attractive and profitable to the non-classical student will have been opened to him by the careful work of the mediators between the old and the new. He will then be enabled to enjoy his Plato or Lucretius, his Sophocles or Plautus in his own tongue, while he leaves the professional scholar to wander happily among the solitudes of their *ipsissima verba* with all concomitant Notes, *Variae Lectiones*, Critical Appendices, and the like.

There is, however, another type of reader who forms a link between these two extremes. Midway between the scholar whose business it is to bring down wreaths from Helicon, and the wide circle before which they are thus conveniently displayed, stands the young disciple of the classicists, to whom the waters of Castalia are often more bitter than Marah itself. I refer to the college undergraduate. He comes from school with a suspicion lurking in his subconscious mind that the works of Caesar and Cicero, if not composed as a kind of intellectual sieve by the College Entrance Board, at least were never written for any end but that lamented by Horace himself, to serve as fodder for the classroom machine. However excellent the teacher, the fact remains that his pilgrims in school have to progress within a specified time through a specified amount of classical literature if they would pass the lions that guard the Palace of Discretion. There is therefore little opportunity for that dallying over points of interest in the calm, unhurried way which should be possible in the college—the *schola*, or place of leisure, as the ancients called it. Yet only thus may the dry bones of Gerund and Gerundive be inspired with the breath of human life and those names which adorn our catalogues of study become in our imagination men and women who did once in truth think and feel and work and play as they do now-a-days.

And such, preëminently, was Catullus. For he was young and faced life with a passionate anticipation of the joy which surely was to be his in Lesbia; in words that have all the simplicity of quick feeling he poured out the story of his love, its rapture and its despair. The *Aeneid* is the poetry of the man who has lived and suffered and endured, who can afford to wait while he clothes his tale in the beautiful artificiality of Roman verse. For those who can read it as a whole its splendour grows with every reading; but it is difficult to realize its beauty when (with eye on Vocabulary) one writhes through the appointed daily dozen lines. Horace is exquisite in form for those who revel in Asclepiads and Alcaics, but our *virgines puerique* are an uninitiated crowd and find it hard to pass the fog of mythology into the poetry above. The short lyrics of Catullus easily reach the understanding and the heart, the more easily because, unlike Vergil or Horace, he reveals himself openly as though conscious of no audience. It is the story of human life which appears in these bursts of love and hatred, of laughter and wit, of satire and reproach, all succeeding one another as rapidly in his little book as they rushed one on another in his brief span of years.

This humanity of Catullus Professor Harrington has pictured for general readers in tracing his influence on literature; my attempt to trace this influence on English-speaking poets is offered to College students in the hope that they may realize more keenly what Catullus has meant through the centuries, and still means, to poets and men of letters. For this reason I have given the English poems in detail and in order of time and I have not hesitated to include translations, if these have served my purpose. Explanations, criticisms, and appreciations I have not included; I leave these to the student and to the professor, who may use these poems for illustration *ex cathedra*. The line of writers runs from Skelton to some now living; I remember the flash of interest on a Freshman's face when she heard that Edna St. Vincent Millay was concerned with Catullus. Some of the passages, like those of Herrick, are reminiscent of Catullus in affection, but not in spirit; for not many poets can reach his union of depth of feeling with height of artistic grace. Some of them cannot claim to have been inspired by him, but tell the same tale. Most of them I have gathered here and there from editions, translations, and books on Catullus; a considerable number have been quoted or mentioned in Professor Harrington's book (Series: *Our Debt to Greece and Rome*), published 1923, and in my article in the *Classical Weekly*, (April 24, 1922). Acknowledgment is due to the Editor of that periodical for permission to use this material and to Messrs. Heath and Company for permission to draw my Latin text from the edition issued by them for Freshman classes in 1924. To the following authors and publishers I am indebted for permission to reprint poems: Mr. Franklin P. Adams and Messrs. Doubleday, Page and Company (*To Furius on Poverty*, from *Weights and Measures*, 1917); Messrs. Dodd, Mead and Company (Mr. Arthur C. Benson, *The Sparrow*, from Poems, 1909: Mr. Arthur Symons, *Lesbia in Old Age; Your honeyed eyes, Juventius; If living sorrows any boon*, from *Knave of Hearts*, 1894-1908); Mr. Laurence Binyon and The Macmillan Company (*Sirmione*, from *Selected Poems*, 1922); The Macmillan Company (Browning, *The Ring and the Book*, XII, lines 277ff.); Messrs. Charles Scribner's Sons (Eugene Field, *Catullus to Lesbia*, from *The Second Book of Verse*, 1896: George Meredith, lines from *Phaëthôn*); Messrs. Martin Secker and Company (James Elroy Flecker, translation of *Carmen* 4, and *Epithalamion*, from *Collected Poems*, 1916); Miss Edna St. Vincent Millay and Messrs. Harper and Brothers, (lines from *Passer mortuus est*, from *Second April*, 1921); *The Living Age* (Mr. J. C. Squire, *To a Roman*, reprinted in *The Living Age*, April 28, 1923); Messrs. Harper and Brothers (Swinburne, *To Catullus* from *A Century of Roundels* and lines from *Dolores*, *Aueatque Vale; In memory of Charles Baudelaire*, "*Insularum Ocelle*," and *Song for the Centenary of Walter Savage Landor*, from Volumes I, III, and V of the *Poems of Charles Algernon Swinburne*, 1904). With regard to my own part in this enterprise, I give warm thanks to President William Allan Neilson, who read and criticized the work in manuscript, and to Professor Florence Alden Gragg, whose *stilus saepe versus* has rescued these pages from innumerable infelicities and errors.

Northampton, Massachusetts,
June, 1925.

Carmen 1.

Cui dono lepidum novum libellum
arida modo pumice expolitum?
Corneli, tibi: namque tu solebas
meas esse aliquid putare nugas,
iam tum cum ausus es unus Italorum
omne aevum tribus explicare chartis
doctis, Iuppiter! et laboriosis.
Quare habe tibi quidquid hoc libelli
qualecumque; quod, o patrona virgo,
plus uno maneat perenne saeclo.

ANDREW LANG, *Ballads of Books*, 1888

Catullus to his Book

My little book, that's neat and new,
Fresh polished with dry pumice stone,
To whom, Cornelius, but to you,
Shall *this* be sent, for you alone—
(Who used to praise my lines, my own)—
Have dared, in weighty volumes three,
(What labours, Jove, what learning thine!)
To tell the Tale of Italy,
And all the legend of our line.

So take, whate'er its worth may be,
My Book,—but, Lady and Queen of Song,
This one kind gift I crave of thee,
That it may live for ages long!

Carmen 2.

Passer, deliciae meae puellae,
quicum ludere, quem in sinu tenere,
cui primum digitum dare appetenti
et acris solet incitare morsus,
cum desiderio meo nitenti
carum nescio quid libet iocari,
et solaciolum sui doloris,
credo, ut tum gravis adquiescat ardor:
tecum ludere sicut ipsa possem
et tristis animi levare curas!
Tam gratum est mihi quam ferunt puellae
pernici aureolum fuisse malum,
quod zonam soluit diu ligatam.

GEORGE GASCOIGNE, *Posies*, 1575—*Weeds*

The Praise of Philip Sparrow

Of all the birds that I do know,
Philip my Sparrow hath no peer:
For sit she high, or lie she low,
Be she far off, or be she near,
There is no bird so fair, so fine,
Nor yet so fresh as this of mine.

Come in a morning merrily,
When Philip hath been lately fed,
Or in an evening soberly,
When Philip list to go to bed:
It is a heaven to hear my Phip,
How she can chirp with cheery lip.

She never wanders far abroad,
But is at hand when I do call,
If I command she lays on load,
With lips, with teeth, with tongue and all:
She chants, she chirps, she makes such cheer,
That I believe she hath no peer.

And yet besides all this good sport,
My Philip can both sing and dance,
With new found toys of sundry sort,
My Philip can both prick and prance:
As if you say but "Fend cut Phip,"
Lord how the pet will turn and skip.

Her feathers are so fresh of hue,
And so well pruned every day,
She lacks none oil, I warrant you,
To trim her tail both trick and gay:
And though her mouth be somewhat wide,
Her tongue is sweet and short beside.

And for the rest I dare compare,
She is both tender, sweet, and soft:
She never lacketh dainty fare,
But is well fed and feedeth oft;
For if my Phip have list to eat,
I warrant you Phip lacks no meat.

And then if that her meat be good,
And such as like do love alway:
She will lay lips thereon, by the rood,
And see that none be cast away:
For when she once hath felt a fit,
Philip will cry still yet, yet, yet.

And to tell truth he were to blame,
Which had so fine a bird as she;
To make him all this goodly game,
Without suspect or jealousy:
He were a churl and knew no good,
Would see her faint for lack of food.

Wherefore I sing and ever shall,
To praise as I have often prov'd,
There is no bird amongst them all,
So worthy for to be belov'd.
Let other praise what bird they will,
Sweet Philip shall be my bird still.

From *Pasquil's Night-Cap or Antidote for the Head-Ache,* 1612

(Grosart, *Occasional Issues,* vol. 4, p. 103.)

But as for Skelton with his Laurel Crowne,
Whose ruffling rimes are emptie quite of marrow:
Or fond Catullus, which set grossely downe
The commendation of a sillie Sparrow;
    Because their lines are void of estimation,
    I passe them over without confutation.
    Much would the Cuckoe thinke herselfe impared
    If shee with Philip Sparrow were compared.

Carmen 3.

Lugete, o Veneres Cupidinesque
et quantum est hominum venustiorum.
Passer mortuus est meae puellae,
passer, deliciae meae puellae,
quem plus illa oculis suis amabat:
nam mellitus erat suamque norat
ipsam tam bene quam puella matrem.
Nec sese a gremio illius movebat,
sed circumsiliens modo huc modo illuc
ad solam dominam usque pipiabat.
Qui nunc it per iter tenebricosum
illud, unde negant redire quemquam.
At vobis male sit, malae tenebrae
Orci, quae omnia bella devoratis!
Tam bellum mihi passerem abstulistis.
O factum male! Io miselle passer!
Tua nunc opera meae puellae
flendo turgiduli rubent ocelli.

JOHN SKELTON (1460?–1529)

From *The Boke of Phyllyp Sparowe*

Whan I remembre agayn
How mi Philyp was slayn,
Never halfe the payne
Was betwene you twayne,
Pyramus and Thesbe,
As than befell to me:
I wept and I wayled,
The tearys downe hayled;
But nothynge it avayled
To call Phylyp agayne,
Whom Gyb our cat hath slayne.

. . . .

It was so prety a fole,
It wold syt on a stole,
And lerned after my scole
For to kepe his cut,
With, Phyllyp, kepe your cut!
It had a velvet cap,
And wold syt upon my lap,
And seke after small wormes,
And somtyme white bred crommes;
And many tymes and ofte
Betwene my brestes softe
It wolde lye and rest;
It was propre and prest.

. . . .

And whan I sayd, Phyp, Phyp,
Than he wold lepe and skyp,
And take me by the lyp.
Alas, it wyll me slo,
That Phillyp is gone me fro!

. . . .

That vengeaunce I aske and crye,
By way of exclamacyon,
On all the hole nacyon
Of cattes wylde and tame;
God send them sorowe and shame!

That cat specyally
That slew so cruelly
My lytell prety sparowe
That I brought up at Carowe.

RICHARD BROME, *Northern Lass*, 1632

From the *Song of Constance*

A bonny bonny Bird I had,
  A Bird that was my Marrow;
A Bird whose pastime made me glad,
  And Philip 'twas my Sparrow.
A pretty Play-fere: Chirp it would,
  And hop, and fly to fist,
Keep cut, as 'twere a Usurers Gold,
  And bill me when I list.
    Philip, Philip, Philip it cryes,
    But he is fled, and my joy dyes.

WILLIAM DRUMMOND OF HAWTHORNDEN (1585-1649)

Upon the death of a linnet

If cruel Death had ears,
Or could be pleas'd by songs,
This wing'd musician liv'd had many years,
And Chloris mine had never wept these wrongs:
For when it first took breath,
The heavens their notes did unto it bequeath;
And, if that Samian's sentence be found true,
Amphion in this body liv'd of new:
But Death, for that he nothing spares, nought hears,
As he doth kings, it kill'd, O grief! O tears!

Phyllis, on the death of her Sparrow

Ah! if ye ask, my friends, why this salt shower
My blubber'd eyes upon this paper pour?
Gone is my sparrow; he whom I did train,
And turn'd so toward, by a cat is slain.
No more with trembling wings shall he attend

His watchful mistress: would my life could end!
No more shall I him hear chirp pretty lays;
Have I not cause to loath my tedious days?
A Daedalus he was to catch a fly,
Nor wrath nor raucour men in him could spy;
To touch or wrong his tail if any dar'd,
He pinch'd their fingers, and against them warr'd:
Then might that crest be seen shake up and down,
Which fixed was unto his little crown;
Like Hector's, Troy's strong bulwark, when in ire
He rag'd to set the Grecian fleet on fire.
But, ah, alas! a cat this prey espies,
Then with a leap did thus our joys surprise.
Undoubtedly this bird was kill'd by treason,
Or otherways had of that fiend had reason.
Thus was Achilles by weak Paris slain,
And stout Camilla fell by Aruns vain:
So that false horse, which Pallas rais'd 'gainst Troy,
King Priam and that city did destroy.
Thou now, whose heart is big with this frail glory,
Shalt not live long to tell thy honour's story.
If any knowledge resteth after death
In ghosts of birds, when they have left to breathe,
My darling's ghost shall know in lower place,
The vengeance falling on the cattish race.
For never cat nor catling I shall find,
But mew shall they in Pluto's palace blind.
Ye who with gaudy wings and bodies light
Do dint the air, turn hitherwards your flight,
To my sad tears comply these notes of yours,
Unto his idol bring an harv'st of flowers;
Let him accept from us, as most divine,
Sabaean incense, milk, food, sweetest wine;
And on a stone let us these words engrave:
"Pilgrim, the body of a sparrow brave
In a fierce gluttonous cat's womb clos'd remains,
Whose ghost now graceth the Elysian plains."

WILLIAM CARTWRIGHT (1611-1643)

Lesbia on her Sparrow

Tell me not of joy! There's none;
Now my little Sparrow's gone!
    He, just as you,
    Would toy and woo!
He would chirp and flatter me!
He would hang the wing a while
Till, at length, he saw me smile.
Lord! how sullen he would be!

He would catch a crumb, and then
Sporting let it go again,
    He from my lip
    Would moisture sip,
He would from my trencher feed,
Then would hop, and then would run
And cry *Philip* when h' had done,
O, whose heart can choose but bleed?

O how eager would he fight
And ne'er hurt though he bite:
    No morn did pass
    But on my glass
He would sit and mark and do
What I did, now ruffle all
His feathers o'er, now let 'em fall
And then straightway sleek them too.

Whence will Cupid get his darts
Feathered now to pierce our hearts?
    A wound he may
    Not love convey.
Now this faithful bird is gone,
O let mournful turtles join
With loving red-breasts, and combine,
    To sing dirges o'er his stone.

ROBERT HERRICK (1591-1674)

From *Upon the death of his Sparrow. An Elegie*

Phill, the late dead, the late dead Deare,
O! may no eye distill a Teare
For you once lost, who weep not here!
Had *Lesbia* (too-too-kind) but known
This Sparrow, she had scorn'd her own:
And for this dead which under-lies,
Wept out her heart, as well as eyes.
But endlesse Peace, sit here, and keep
My *Phill*, the time he has to sleep,
And thousand Virgins come and weep—

MATTHEW PRIOR (1664-1721)

From *The Turtle and Sparrow* (The Sparrow is doing his best to cheer the widow dove, Turturella, inconsolable for the loss of her mate, Colombo).

Whate'er Pythagoras may say
(For each, you know, will have his way)
With great submission I pronounce,
That people die no more than once.
But once is sure; and death is common
To bird and man, including woman;
From the spread eagle to the wren,
Alas! no mortal fowl knows when;
All that wear feathers first or last
Must one day perch on Charon's mast;
Must lie beneath the cypress shade,
Where Strada's nightingale was laid;
Those fowl who seem alive to sit,
Assembled by Dan Chaucer's wit,
In prose have slept three hundred years,
Exempt from worldly hopes and fears,
And, laid in state upon their hearse
Are truly but embalmed in verse.
As sure as Lesbia's sparrow I,
Thou sure as Prior's dove, must die,
And ne'er again from Lethe's streams,
Return to Adige, or to Thames.

SIR C. HANBURY WILLIAMS (1708-1759)

From the *Ode on the Death of Matzel, a favorite bullfinch.*

Matzel's no more; ye Graces, Loves,
Ye linnets, nightingales, and doves,
  Attend th' untimely bier;
Let every sorrow be exprest,
Beat with your wings each mournful breast,
  And drop each nat'ral tear.

. . . .

In vain I lov'd, in vain I mourn
My bird, who never to return
  Is fled to happier shades,
Where Lesbia shall for him prepare
The place most charming, and most fair,
  Of all th' Elysian glades.

WILLIAM COWPER (1731-1800)

From *On the death of Mrs. Throckmorton's Bullfinch*

Ye Nymphs! if e'er your eyes were red
With tears o'er hapless favourites shed,
  O share Maria's grief!
Her favourite, even in his cage
(What will not hunger's cruel rage?)
  Assassin'd by a thief . . .

Epitaph on a Free but Tame Redbreast

These are not dewdrops, these are tears,
  And tears by Sally shed,
For absent Robin, who she fears
  With too much cause, is dead.

One morn he came not to her hand
  As he was wont to come,
And, on her finger perch'd, to stand
  Picking his breakfast crumb.

Alarm'd, she call'd him and perplex'd
She sought him, but in vain;
That day he came not, nor the next,
Nor ever came again.

She therefore raised him here a tomb,
Though where he fell or how,
None knows, so secret was his doom,
Nor where he moulders now.

Had half a score of coxcombs died
In social Robin's stead,
Poor Sally's tears had soon been dried.
Or haply never shed.

But Bob was neither rudely bold,
Nor spiritlessly tame;
Nor was, like theirs, his bosom cold,
But always in a flame.

SYLVESTER DOUGLAS, BARON GLENBERVIE (1743-1823)

From *Occasional verses, Translations and Imitations*
On the death of a young bullfinch, 1775

Farewell, sweet bird! and art thou dead?
Thy voice extinct, thy spirit fled!
O, loss beyond repair!
Could naught avail? the tears of Fan?
Thy soft caresses, gentle Ann?
Nor all my anxious care?

. . . .

Thee, gentle Ann had call'd her own,
Her alabaster hand thy throne,
Her breast had been thy nest:
And sure a mistress so divine,
So tender and so fair as thine,
No bullfinch e'er possess'd.

But peace be with thy lovely shade!
The grave no plough shall e'er invade;
    And each revolving year,
In silent grief shall Ann and I,
While plaintive turtles murmur nigh,
    Bedew thee with a tear.

WILLIAM WORDSWORTH (1770-1850)

To.........., 1835

"Wait, prithee, wait!" this answer Lesbia threw
Forth to her Dove, and took no further heed;
Her eye was busy, while her fingers flew
Across the harp, with soul-engrossing speed;
But from that bondage when her thoughts were freed
She rose, and toward the close-shut casement drew,
Whence the poor unregarded Favourite, true
To old affections, had been heard to plead
With flapping wing for entrance. What a shriek!
Forced from that voice so lately tuned to a strain
Of harmony!—a shriek of terror, pain,
And self-reproach! for, from aloft, a Kite
Pounced,—and the Dove, which from its ruthless beak
She could not rescue, perished in her sight!

ALFRED TENNYSON (1809-1892)

From *Poets and their Bibliographies*

Old poets foster'd under friendlier skies,
    Old Virgil who would write ten lines, they say,
    At dawn, and lavish all the golden day
To make them wealthier in his readers' eyes;
And you, old popular Horace, you the wise
    Adviser of the nine-years-ponder'd lay,
    And you, that wear a wreath of sweeter bay,
Catullus whose dead songster never dies; . . .

ROBERT BROWNING (1812-1889)

From *The Ring and the Book*, XII, 270ff.[1]

Thus
Came the Count to his end of gallant man,
Defunct in faith and exemplarity:
Nor shall the shield of his great House lose shine
Thereby, nor its blue banner blush to red.
This, too, should yield sustainment to our hearts—
He had commiseration and respect
In his decease from universal Rome,
Quantum est hominum venustiorum,
The nice and cultivated everywhere:

A. C. BENSON, *Poems*, 1909

From *The Sparrow*

O pertest, most self-satisfied
Of aught that breathes or moves,
See where you sit, with head aside,
To chirp your vulgar loves:
Or raking in the uncleanly street
You bolt your ugly meal,
Undaunted by the approaching feet,
The heedless splashing wheel.

Old poets in your praise were stirred—
I fear you must forget—
Catullus loved you, shameless bird,
You were his lady's pet.
You heard her dainty breathing, perched
Beside her when she slept;
You died:—her pretty cheeks were smirched;—
And 'twas for you she wept.

[1] Globe Edition of Browning. Copyright (1921) by The Macmillan Company. Reprinted here by permission.

EDMUND GOSSE, (1849-)

Villanelle

Little mistress mine good-bye!
    I have been your sparrow true;
Dig my grave, for I must die.

Waste no tear, and heave no sigh;
    Life should still be blithe for you,
Little mistress mine, good-bye!

In your garden let me lie
    Underneath the pointed yew,
Dig my grave, for I must die.

We have loved the quiet sky
    With its tender arch of blue;
Little mistress mine, good-bye!

That I still may feel you nigh,
    In your virgin bosom, too,
Dig my grave, for I must die.

Let our garden friends that fly
    Be the mourners, fit and few.
Little mistress mine, good-bye!
    Dig my grave, for I must die.

EDNA ST. VINCENT MILLAY (1892-)

From *Passer Mortuus est*

Death devours all lovely things;
    Lesbia with her sparrow
Shares the darkness,—presently
    Every bed is narrow

Unremembered as old rain
    Dries the sheer libation
And the little petulant hand
    Is an annotation . . .

Anonymous, quoted by H. W. GARROD, *The Oxford Book of Latin Verse*, 1912, p. 454.

Weep, weep, ye Loves and Cupids all,
And ilka Man o'decent feelin':
My lassie's lost her wee, wee bird,
And that's a loss, ye'll ken, past healin'.

The lassie lo'ed him like her een:
The darling wee thing lo'ed the ither,
And knew and nestled to her breast,
As ony bairnie to her mither.

Her bosom was his dear, dear haunt—
So dear, he cared na lang to leave it;
He'd nae but gang his ain sma' jaunt,
And flutter piping back bereavit.

The wee thing's gane the shadowy road
That's never travelled back by ony:
Out on ye, Shades! ye're greedy aye
To grab at aught that's brave and bonny.

Puir, foolish, fondling, bonnie bird,
Ye little ken what wark ye're leavin':
Ye've gar'd my lassie's een grow red,
Those bonnie een grow red wi' grievin'.

Carmen 4.

Phasellus ille quem videtis, hospites,
ait fuisse navium celerrimus,
neque ullius natantis impetum trabis
nequisse praeterire, sive palmulis
opus foret volare sive linteo.
Et hoc negat minacis Hadriatici
negare litus insulasve Cycladas
Rhodumque nobilem horridamque Thraciam,
Propontida trucemque Ponticum sinum,
ubi iste, post phasellus, antea fuit
comata silva: nam Cytorio in iugo
loquente saepe sibilum edidit coma.
Amastri Pontica et Cytore buxifer,
tibi haec fuisse et esse cognitissima
ait phasellus: ultima ex origine
tuo stetisse dicit in cacumine,
tuo imbuisse palmulas in aequore,
et inde tot per impotentia freta
erum tulisse, laeva sive dextera
vocaret aura, sive utrumque Iuppiter
simul secundus incidisset in pedem.
Neque ulla vota litoralibus deis
sibi esse facta, cum veniret a mari
novissime hunc ad usque limpidum lacum.
Sed haec prius fuere; nunc recondita
senet quiete seque dedicat tibi,
gemelle Castor et gemelle Castoris.

JAMES ELROY FLECKER (1884-1915)

Proud is Phaselus here, my friends, to tell
That once she was the swiftest craft afloat:
No vessel, were she winged with blade or sail,
Could ever pass my boat.
Phaselus shunned to shun grim Adria's shore,
Or Cyclades, or Rhodes the wide renowned,
Or Bosphorus, where Thracian waters roar,
Or Pontus' eddying sound.
It was in Pontus once, unwrought, she stood,
And conversed, sighing, with her sister trees,
Amastris born, or where Cytorus' wood
Answers the mountain breeze.
Pontic Amastris, boxwood-clad Cytorus!—
You, says Phaselus, are her closest kin:
Yours were the forests where she stood inglorious:
The waters yours wherein
She dipped her virgin blades; and from your strand
She bore her master through the cringing straits,
Nought caring were the wind on either hand,
Or whether kindly fates
Filled both the straining sheets. Never a prayer
For her was offered to the gods of haven,
Till last she left the sea, hither to fare,
And to be lightly laven
By the cool ripple of the clear lagoon.
. . . .
This too is past; at length she is allowed
Long slumber through her life's long afternoon,
To Castor and the twin of Castor vowed.

HUMMEL AND BRODRIBB, *Lays from Latin Lyres*, 1876

This ship you see by Salter's raft
Boasts that she was the fleetest craft
    That ever Isis knew;
For three years in the summer race
First on the stream she kept her place,
So unapproachable her pace,
    So lusty were her crew.
What vanquished rival can deny
Her prowess, or presume to vie
    With laurels such as these?
Can Christchurch proud such honour claim,
Or Brasenose of boating fame,
Or Exeter with crimson oar,
Or Balliol men from Scotia's shore?
    There, 'midst a clump of trees,
A noble pine of haughty birth
Disdained to speak with Mother Earth,
    But whispered to the breeze:
This was my heroine, foully slain,
Brought from the mountain to the main,
Whence, many a storm and peril past,
She reached the quiet Thames at last,
And, deftly shaped and set afloat,
Became an outrigged racing boat.
Strange history! now her life is done,
Her very occupation gone,
And laid aside, she feels no more
The throbbing pulses of the oar,
But ages in serener state,
To the Twin Brethren consecrate.

Carmen 5.

Vivamus, mea Lesbia, atque amemus,
rumoresque senum severiorum
omnes unius aestimemus assis.
Soles occidere et redire possunt;
nobis cum semel occidit brevis lux,
nox est perpetua una dormienda.
Da mi basia mille, deinde centum,
dein mille altera, dein secunda centum,
deinde usque altera mille, deinde centum;
dein, cum milia multa fecerimus,
conturbabimus illa, ne sciamus
aut ne quis malus invidere possit
cum tantum sciat esse basiorum.

CHRISTOPHER MARLOWE (1564-1593)

The Passionate Shepherd to his Love

Come live with me and be my love,
And we will all the pleasures prove
That hills and valleys, dales and fields,
Woods or steepy mountain yields.

And we will sit upon the rocks,
Seeing the shepherds feed their flocks
By shallow rivers, to whose falls
Melodious birds sing madrigals.

And I will make thee beds of roses
And a thousand fragrant posies,
A cap of flowers, and a kirtle
Embroidered all with leaves of myrtle;

A gown made of the finest wool,
Which from our pretty lambs we pull;
Fair-linèd slippers for the cold,
With buckles of the purest gold;

A belt of straw and ivy-buds,
With coral clasps and amber studs:
And if these pleasures may thee move,
Come live with me and be my love.

The shepherd swains shall dance and sing
For thy delight each May morning:
If these delights thy mind may move,
Then live with me and be my love.

THOMAS CAMPION (1567?-1619)

From *A Booke of Ayres*

My sweetest Lesbia let us live and love,
And though the sager sort our deedes reprove,
Let us not way them: heav'ns great lampes doe dive
Into their west, and strait againe revive,
But soone as once set is our little light,
Then must we sleepe one ever-during night.

GEORGE CHAPMAN (1559?-1634)

From *The Blind Beggar of Alexandria*

Count But come sweete love if thou wilt come with me,
We two will live amongst the shadowy groves,
And we will sit like shepherdes on a hill,
And with our heavenly voyces tice the trees,
To eccho sweetely to our coelestiall tunes.
Else will I angle in the running brookes,
Seasoning our toyles with kisses on the bankes;
Sometime Ile dive into the murmering springes,
And fetch thee stones to hang about thy necke,
Which by thy splendor will be turnd to pearle,
Say, fayre *Aspasia*, wilt thou walke with me?
Aspasia No, bloody *Count*, but I will cleare myself,
And tell thy murders to the amased court.
Count Nay, if thou wilt not chuse, you peevish girle, . . .

JOHN DONNE (1573-1631)

From *The Baite*

Come live with me, and bee my love,
And we will some new pleasures prove
Of golden sands, and christall brookes,
With silken lines, and silver hookes.

From *A Valediction: forbidding mourning*

So let us melt, and make no noise,
No tear-floods, nor sigh-tempests move,
T'were prophanation of our joyes
To tell the layetie our love.

Ben Jonson (1573?-1637)

From *The Fox*, III, 6

Volpone. Come, my Celia, let us prove,
While we can, the sports of love;
Time will not be ours for ever:
He at length our good will sever.
Spend not then his gifts in vain:
Suns that set, may rise again;
But if once we lose this light,
'Tis with us perpetual night.
Why should we defer our joys?
Fame and rumour are but toys.
Cannot we delude the eyes
Of a few poor household spies?
Or his easier ears beguile,
Thus removed by our wile?
'Tis no sin love's fruits to steal,
But the sweet thefts to reveal;
To be taken, to be seen,
These have crimes accounted been.

Thomas Carew (c. 1598-1639)

From *Perswasions to Love*

O love me then, and now begin it,
Let us not loose this present minute;
For time and age will worke that wrack
Which time and age shall ne're call backe.
The snake each yeare fresh skin resumes,
And eagles change their aged plumes;
The faded rose each spring receives
A fresh red tincture on her leaves:
But if your beauties once decay,
You nere shall know a second May.
O then be wise, and whilst your season
Affords you dayes for sport, doe reason;
Spend not in vaine your lives short houre,
But crop in time your beautie's flower,
Which will away, and doth together
Both bud and fade, both blow and wither.

From *The Complement*

O my deerest, I shall grieve thee
When I sweare, yet (sweete) beleeve me:
By thine eyes, that crystall brooke
On which crabbed old age looke,
I sweare to thee, (though none abhorre them)
Yet I do not love thee for them . . . .

WILLIAM DRUMMOND OF HAWTHORNDEN (1585-1649)

To Thaumantia

Come, let us live and love,
And kiss, Thaumantia mine:
I shall the elm be, be to me the vine;
Come let us teach new billing to the dove;
Nay, to augment our bliss,
Let souls even other kiss;
Let Love a workman be,
Undo, distemper, and his cunning prove,
Of kisses three make one, of one make three:
Though moon, sun, stars, be bodies far more bright,
Let them not vaunt they match us in delight.

Kisses Desired

Though I with strange desire
To kiss those rosy lips am set on fire,
Yet will I cease to crave
Sweet touches in such store,
As he who long before
From Lesbia them in thousands did receive.
Heart mine, but once me kiss,
And I by that sweet bliss
Even swear to cease you to importune more:
Poor one no number is;
Another word of me ye shall not hear
After one kiss, but still one kiss, my dear.

RICHARD CRASHAW (1613?-1649)

Out of Catullus

Come and let us live my deare,
Let us love and never feare,
What the sowrest fathers say:
Brightest Sol that dyes to day
Lives againe as blith to morrow;
But if we darke sons of sorrow
Set: O then how long a Night
Shuts the eyes of our short light!
Then let amorous kisses dwell
On our lips, begin and tell
A thousand, and a hundred score,
An hundred and a thousand more,
Till another thousand smother
That, and that wipe off another.
Thus at last when we have numbred
Many a thousand, many a hundred,
Wee'l confound the reckoning quite
And lose our selves in wild delight:
While our joyes so multiply
As shall mocke the envious eye.

EDMUND WALLER, *Poems upon several Occasions,* 1645

To Phyllis

Phyllis, why should we delay
Pleasures shorter than the day?
Could we (which we never can)
Stretch our lives beyond their span,
Beauty like a shadow flies,
And our youth before us dies;
Or, would youth and beauty stay,
Love hath wings, and will away.
Love hath swifter wings than Time:
Change in love to heaven does climb;
Gods, that never change their state,
Vary oft their love and hate.

Phyllis, to this truth we owe
All the love betwixt us two.
Let nòt you and I enquire
What has been our past desire;
On what shepherds you have smiled,
Or what nymphs I have beguiled;
Leave it to the planets too,
What we shall hereafter do:
For the joys we now may prove,
Take advice of present love.

ROBERT HERRICK (1591-1674)

Kissing Usurie

Biancha, Let
Me pay the debt
I owe thee for a kisse
Thou lend'st to me;
And I to thee
Will render ten for this:

If thou wilt say,
Ten will not pay
For that so rich a one;
Ile cleare the summe,
If it will come
Unto a Million.

By this, I guesse,
Of happinesse
Who has a little measure:
He must of right,
To th'utmost mite,
Make payment for his pleasure.

From *To Anthea*

Ah my *Anthea*! Must my heart still break?
(Love makes me write, what shame forbids to speak.)
Give me a kisse, and to that kisse a score;
Then to that twenty, adde an hundred more:
A thousand to that hundred: so kisse on,
To make that thousand up a million.

Treble that million, and when that is done,
Let's kisse afresh, as when we first begun . . . .

From *Corinna's going a Maying*

Come, let us goe, while we are in our prime;
And take the harmlesse follie of the time.
We shall grow old apace, and die
Before we know our liberty.
Our life is short; and our dayes run
As fast away as do's the Sunne:
And as a vapour, or a drop of raine
Once lost, can ne'r be found againe:
So when or you or I are made
A fable, song, or fleeting shade;
All love, all liking, all delight
Lies drown'd with us in endlesse night.
Then while time serves, and we are but decaying;
Come, my *Corinna*, come, let's goe a Maying.

From *To Phillis to love, and live with him*

Live, live with me, and thou shalt see
The pleasures Ile prepare for thee:
What sweets the Country can afford
Shall blesse thy Bed, and blesse thy Board.
. . . .
These (nay) and more, thine own shal be,
If thou wilt love, and live with me.

SIR RICHARD FANSHAWE (1608-1666)

Of Beauty

Let us use it while we may,
Snatch those joys that haste away!
Earth her winter coat may cast,
And renew her beauty past;
But, our winter come, in vain
We solicit Spring again;
And when our furrows snow shall cover
Love may return, but never lover.

ANDREW MARVELL (1621-1678)

From *To his Coy Mistress*

Now therefore while the youthful hue
Sits on thy skin like morning dew,
And while thy willing soul transpires
At every pore with instant fires,
Now let us sport us while we may,
And now, like amorous birds of prey,
Rather at once our time devour
Than languish in his slow-chapt power.
Let us roll all our strength, and all
Our sweetness up into one ball;
And tear our pleasures with rough strife
Thorough the iron gates of life:
Thus, though we cannot make our sun
Stand still, yet we will make him run.

GEORGE MONCK BERKELEY (1763-1793)

Can love be controll'd by advice,
  Can madness and reason agree?
O Molly, who'd ever be wise,
  If madness is loving of thee?
Let sages pretend to despise
  The joys they want spirits to taste,
Let us seize old time as he flies,
  And the blessings of life while they last.
Dull wisdom but adds to our cares;
  Brisk love will improve ev'ry joy,
Too soon we may meet with gray hairs,
  Too late may repent being coy.
Then, Molly, for what should we stay
  Till our best blood begins to run cold?
Our youth we can have but to-day,
  We may always find time to grow old.

John Langhorne (1735-1779)

Lesbia, live to love and pleasure,
  Careless what the grave may say:
When each moment is a treasure
  Why should lovers lose a day?

Setting suns shall rise in glory,
  But when little life is o'er,
There's an end of all the story—
  We shall sleep, and wake no more.

Give me, then, a thousand kisses,
  Twice ten thousand more bestow,
Till the sum of boundless blisses
  Neither we nor envy know.

Samuel Taylor Coleridge, *Imitations*, 1798

To Lesbia

My Lesbia, let us love and live,
And to the winds, my Lesbia, give
Each cold restraint, each boding fear
Of age and all her saws severe.
Yon sun now posting to the main
Will set—but 'tis to rise again:—
But we, when once our mortal light
Is set, must sleep in endless night!
Then come, with whom alone I'll live,
A thousand kisses take and give!
Another thousand! to the store
Add hundreds—then a thousand more!
And when they to a million mount,
Let confusion take the account,—
That you, the number never knowing,
May continue still bestowing—
That I for joys may never pine,
Which never can again be mine!

GEORGE GORDON BYRON, LORD BYRON (1788-1824)

To Ellen, 1806

Oh! might I kiss those eyes of fire,
A million scarce would quench desire:
Still would I steep my lips in bliss,
And dwell an age on every kiss:
Nor then my soul should sated be,
Still would I kiss and cling to thee:
Nought should my kiss from thine dissever,
Still would we kiss and kiss for ever;
E'en though the numbers did exceed
The yellow harvest's countless seed.
To part would be a vain endeavour:
Could I desist? ah! never—never!

EUGENE FIELD, *Second Book of Verse,* 1896

Catullus to Lesbia

Come, my Lesbia, no repining;
    Let us love while yet we may!
Suns go on forever shining;
    But when we have had our day,
Sleep perpetual shall o'ertake us,
And no morrow's dawn awake us.

Come, in yonder nook reclining,
        Where the honeysuckle climbs,
Let us mock at Fate's designing,
    Let us kiss a thousand times!
And if they shall prove too few, dear,
When they're kissed we'll start anew, dear!

And should any chance to see us,
    Goodness! how they'll agonize!
How they'll wish that they could be us,
    Kissing in such liberal wise!
Never mind their envious whining;
Come, my Lesbia, no repining!

ROBERT BRIDGES, *New Poems*, No. 7, 1899

I climb the mossy bank of the glade:
My love awaiteth me in the shade.

She holdeth a book that she never heedeth:
In Goddës work her spirit readeth.

She is all to me, and I to her:
When we embrace, the stars confer.

O my love, from beyond the sky
I am calling thy heart, and who but I?

Fresh as love is the breeze of June,
In the dappled shade of the summer noon.

Catullus, throwing his heart away,
Gave fewer kisses every day.

Heracleitus, spending his youth
In search of wisdom, had less of truth.

Flame of fire was the poet's desire:
The thinker found that life was fire.

O my love! my song is done:
My kiss hath both their fires in one.

Carmen 7.

Quaeris quot mihi basiationes
tuae, Lesbia, sint satis superque.
Quam magnus numerus Libyssae harenae
lasarpiciferis iacet Cyrenis,
oraclum Iovis inter aestuosi
et Batti veteris sacrum sepulcrum;
aut quam sidera multa, cum tacet nox,
furtivos hominum vident amores:
tam te basia multa basiare
vesano satis et super Catullo est,
quae nec pernumerare curiosi
possint nec mala fascinare lingua.

THOMAS CAMPION (1567?-1619)

From *The Second Booke of Ayres*

Sooner may you count the starres,
 And number hail down pouring,
Tell the Osiers of the *Temmes*,
 Or *Goodwins* Sands devouring,
Then the thicke-showr'd kisses here
 Which now thy tyred lips must beare.

. . . .

Would it were dumb midnight now,
 When all the world lyes sleeping:
Would this place some Desert were,
 Which no man hath in keeping.

BEN JONSON (1573?-1637)

To Celia

Kiss me, sweet: the wary lover
Can your favours keep, and cover,
When the common courting jay
All your bounties will betray.
Kiss again! no creature comes;
Kiss, and score up wealthy sums
On my lips, thus hardly sundered,
While you breathe. First give a hundred,
Then a thousand, then another
Hundred, then unto the other
Add a thousand, and so more:
Till you equal with the store,
All the grass that Rumney yields,
Or the sands in Chelsea fields,
Or the drops in silver Thames,
Or the stars that gild his streams,
In the silent Summer-nights,
When youths ply their stolen delights;
That the curious may not know
How to tell 'em as they flow,
And the envious, when they find
What their number is, be pined.

JOHN OLDHAM, *Poems and Translations,* 1683

Nay, *Lesbia,* never ask me this,
How many kisses will suffice?
Faith, 'tis a question hard to tell,
Exceeding hard; for you as well
May ask what sums of Gold suffice
The greedy Miser's boundless Wish:
Think what drops the Ocean store,
With all the Sands, that make its Shore:
Think what Spangles deck the Skies,
When Heaven looks with all its Eyes:
Or think how many Atoms came
To compose this mighty Frame:
Let all these the Counters be,
To tell how oft I'm kiss'd by thee:
Till no malicious Spy can guess
To what vast height the Scores arise;
Till weak Arithmetick grow scant,
And numbers for the reck'ning want:
All these will hardly be enough
For me stark staring mad with Love.

SIR EDWARD SHERBURNE (1618-1702)

By a gentle river laid,
Thirsis to his Phillis said:
"Equal to these sandy grains
Is the number of my pains;
And the drops within their bounds
Speak the sum of all my wounds."

Phillis, whom like passion burns,
Thirsis answer thus returns:
"Many as the Earth hath leaves
Are the griefs my heart receives;
And the stars, which Heaven inspires,
Reckon my consuming fires."

Then the shepherd in the pride
Of his happy love reply'd:
"With the choristers of air
Shall our numerous joys compare;
And our mutual pleasures vie
With the Cupids in thy eye."

Thus the willing shepherdess
Did her ready love express:
"In delight our pains shall cease,
And our wars be cured by peace;
We will count our griefs with blisses,
Thousand torments, thousand kisses."

SIR C. HANBURY WILLIAMS (1708-1759)

On Lady Ilchester asking Lord Ilchester how many kisses he would have

Dear Betty, come give me sweet kisses,
For sweeter no girl e'er gave:
But why, in the midst of our blisses,
Do you ask me how many I'd have?
I'm not to be stinted in pleasure;
Then, prithee, dear Betty, be kind,
For, as I love thee beyond measure,

To numbers I'll not be confined.
Count the bees that on Hybla are straying,
Count the flowers that enamel the fields,
Count the flock that on Tempe are playing,
Or the grains that each Sicily yields;
Count how many stars are in heaven,
Go reckon the sands on the shore,
And when so many kisses you've given,
I still shall be asking for more.

Carmen 8.

Miser Catulle, desinas ineptire
et quod vides perisse perditum ducas.
Fulsere quondam candidi tibi soles,
cum ventitabas quo puella ducebat
amata nobis quantum amabitur nulla.
Ibi illa multa tum iocosa fiebant,
quae tu volebas nec puella nolebat.
Fulsere vere candidi tibi soles.
Nunc iam illa non vult; tu quoque, impotens, noli,
nec quae fugit sectare, nec miser vive,
sed obstinata mente perfer, obdura.
Vale, puella: iam Catullus obdurat
nec te requiret nec rogabit invitam.
At tu dolebis, cum rogaberis nulla.
Scelesta, vae te! Quae tibi manet vita!
Quis nunc te adibit? Cui videberis bella?
Quem nunc amabis? Cuius esse diceris?
Quem basiabis? Cui labella mordebis?
At tu, Catulle, destinatus obdura.

THOMAS CAMPION (1567?-1619)

From *The Second Booke of Ayres*

Harden now thy tyred hart, with more then flinty rage;
Ne'er let her false teares henceforth thy constant griefe asswage.
Once true happy dayes thou saw'st when shee stood firme and [kinde,
Both as one then liv'd and held one eare, one tongue, one minde:
But now those bright houres be fled, and never may returne;
What then remaines but her untruths to mourne?

Silly Traytresse, who shall now thy carelesse tresses place?
Who thy pretty talke supply, whose eare thy musicke grace?
Who shall thy bright eyes admire? what lips triumph with thine?
Day by day who'll visit thee and say "th'art onely mine?"
Such a time there was, God wot, but such shall never be:
Too oft, I feare, thou wilt remember me.

SIR ROBERT AYTON (1570-1638)

Inconstancy Reproved

I do confess thou'rt smooth and fair,
And I might have gone near to love thee,
Had I not found the slightest pray'r
That lips could speak, had pow'r to move thee;
But I can let thee now alone,
As worthy to be lov'd by none.

I do confess thou'rt sweet; yet find
Thee such an unthrift of thy sweets,
Thy favours are but like the wind,
Which kisseth everything it meets.
And since thou canst love more than one,
Thou'rt worthy to be kiss'd by none.

. . . .

Such fate, ere long, will thee betide,
When thou hast handled been awhile,
Like fair flowers to be thrown aside;

And thou shalt sigh, when I shall smile
To see thy love to every one
Hath brought thee to be lov'd by none.

ABRAHAM COWLEY (1618-1667)

From *Love Given Over*

It is enough; enough of Time and Pain
Hast thou consum'd in vain;
Leave, wretched Cowley, leave
Thy self with Shadows to deceive;
Think that already lost which thou must never gain.

GEORGE GRANVILLE, LORD LANSDOWNE

From *A Collection of Poems*, 1701

The happiest mortals once were we,
I loved Myra, Myra me;
Each desirous of the blessing,
Nothing wanting but possessing;
I loved Myra, Myra me:
The happiest mortals once were we.
But since cruel fates dissever,
Torn from love, and torn forever,
Tortures end me,
Death befriend me!
Of all pain, the greatest pain
Is to love, and love in vain.

THOMAS COOKE (1703-1756)

To Phillis

Phillis from this hour adieu,
Fair no more, no longer true;
I my wandering heart recall;
Take my vows, I quit them all;
Henceforth thou no more shalt be
Than a vulgar maid to me.

Phillis from this hour adieu,
Fair no more, no longer true.
Why should I, presumptuous swain,
Dare to cherish hopes so vain,
That the heavens would hear my prayer
For a love as chaste as fair.
Phillis thou hast prov'd no more
Than a thousand belles before
Have to men who them believ'd,—
Plighted vows, and then deceived!
Such was Delia to Tibullus,
Lesbia such to fond Catullus.
Horace, sacred bard, complains
Of the sex, and slighted pains.
Phillis thou art free to rove
As the natives of the grove:
From this moment, nymph, adieu,
Fair no more, no longer true.

ARTHUR SYMONS, *Knave of Hearts* (1894-1908)

Lesbia in Old Age

You see these shrunken arms, this chin,
A sharp bone wrapped about with rags
Of scrawled and wrinkled parchment skin;
This neck now puckered into bags
Was seamless satin at the first;
And this dry broken mouth a cup
Filled up with wine for all men's thirst;
This sodden hair was lifted up
In coils that as a crown were curled
About a brow that once was low,
As any woman's in the world;
And these two eyes of smouldering tow
That scarcely light me to this hearth
Were as two torches shaken out
To be a flame upon the earth.

What is it that he said about
Beauty I stole, to be my own,
All beauty's beauty? Look at this:
Finger by finger, to the bone,
His lips and teeth would bite and kiss
These joints of these abhorred hands,
These cheeks that were not always thus;
What was it that he said of sands
And stars that could not count for us
Our kisses? Let us live and love,
My Lesbia: yes, and I shall live,
A hungering, thirsting shadow of
That love I gave and could not give.
I gave him pleasure, and I sold
To him and all men; he is dead,
And I am infamous and old,
And yet I am not quieted.
Take off your curses from my soul:
Can not Catullus pity me
Although my name upon his scroll
Has brought him immortality?

Carmen 10.

Varus me meus ad suos amores
visum duxerat e foro otiosum,
scortillum, ut mihi tunc repente visum est,
non sane inlepidum neque invenustum.
Huc ut venimus, incidere nobis
sermones varii, in quibus, quid esset
iam Bithynia, quo modo se haberet,
ecquonam mihi profuisset aere.
Respondi id quod erat: nihil neque ipsis
nec praetoribus esse nec cohorti,
cur quisquam caput unctius referret,
praesertim quibus esset inrumator
praetor, nec faceret pili cohortem.
"At certe tamen," inquiunt, "quod illic
natum dicitur esse comparasti,
ad lecticam homines." Ego, ut puellae
unum me facerem beatiorem,
"Non," inquam, "mihi tam fuit maligne
ut, provincia quod mala incidisset,
non possem octo homines parare rectos."
At mi nullus erat, neque hic neque illic,
fractum qui veteris pedem grabati
in collo sibi collocare posset.
Hic illa, ut decuit cinaediorem,
"Quaeso," inquit, "mihi, mi Catulle, paulum
istos commoda: nam volo ad Sarapim
deferri." "Mane," inquii puellae,
"istud quod modo dixeram me habere,
fugit me ratio: meus sodalis
Cinna est Gaius; is sibi paravit.
Verum, utrum illius an mei, quid ad me?
Utor tam bene quam mihi pararim.
Sed tu insulsa male et molesta vivis,
per quam non licet esse neglegentem!"

JOHN HOOKHAM FRERE (1769-1846)

Translation

Varus, whom I chanced to meet
The other evening in the street,
Engaged me there, upon the spot,
To see a mistress he had got.
She seem'd, as far as I can gather,
Lively and smart, and handsome rather.
There, as we rested from our walk,
We enter'd into different talk—
As, how much might Bithynia bring?
And had I found it a good thing?
I answer'd, as it was the fact,
The province had been stript and sack'd;
That there was nothing for the praetors,
And still less for us wretched creatures,
His poor companions and toad-eaters.
"At least" says she, "you bought some fellows
To bear your litter; for they tell us,
Our only good ones come from there."
I chose to give myself an air;
"Why, truly, with my poor estate,
The difference wasn't quite so great
Betwixt a province, good or bad,
That where a purchase could be had,
Eight lusty fellows, straight and tall,
I shouldn't find the wherewithal
To buy them." But it was a lie;
For not a single wretch had I—
No single cripple fit to bear
A broken bedstead or a chair.
She, like a strumpet, pert and knowing,
Said—"Dear Catullus, I am going
To worship at Serapis' shrine—
Do lend me, pray, those slaves of thine!"
I answer'd—"It was idly said,—
They were a purchase Cinna made
(Caius Cinna, my good friend)—

It was the same thing in the end,
Whether a purchase or a loan—
I always used them as my own;
Only the phrase was inexact—
He bought them for himself, in fact.
But you have caught the general vice
Of being too correct and nice,
Over curious and precise;
And seizing with precipitation
The slight neglects of conversation."

Carmen 11 (quoted in part)

Furi et Aureli, comites Catulli,
. . . .
pauca nuntiate meae puellae
    non bona dicta.

Cum suis vivat valeatque moechis
quos simul complexa tenet trecentos,
nullum amans vere sed identidem omnium
    ilia rumpens.

Nec meum respectet, ut ante, amorem
qui illius culpa cecidit velut prati
ultimi flos, praetereunte postquam
    tactus aratro est.

THOMAS CAREW (c. 1598-1639)

From *Disdaine returned*

Celia, now, no teares shall win
    My resolv'd heart to returne;
I have searcht thy soule within,
    And find nought but pride and scorne:
I have learn'd thy arts, and now
Can disdaine as much as thou.

ROBERT BURNS (1759-1796)

From *To a Mountain Daisy*
On Turning one down with the Plough, 1786

Wee, modest, crimson-tippèd flow'r,
Thou's met me in an evil hour;
For I maun crush amang the stoure
    Thy slender stem:
To spare thee now is past my pow'r,
    Thou bonie gem.

. . . .

There, in thy scantie mantle clad,
Thy snawie bosom sun-ward spread,
Thou lifts thy unassuming head
    In humble guise;
But now the share uptears thy bed,
    And low thou lies!

. . . .

Ev'n thou who mourn'st the daisy's fate,
That fate is thine—no distant date;
Stern Ruin's ploughshare drives elate,
    Full on thy bloom,
Till crushed beneath the furrow's weight
    Shall be thy doom.

Carmen 12.

Marrucine Asini, manu sinistra
non belle uteris in ioco atque vino:
tollis lintea neglegentiorum.
Hoc salsum esse putas? Fugit te, inepte;
quamvis sordida res et invenusta est.
Non credis mihi? Crede Pollioni
fratri, qui tua furta vel talento
mutari velit: est enim leporum
disertus puer ac facetiarum.
Quare aut hendecasyllabos trecentos
exspecta aut mihi linteum remitte,
quod me non movet aestimatione
verum est mnemosynum mei sodalis.
Nam sudaria Saetaba ex Hiberis
miserunt mihi muneri Fabullus
et Veranius. Haec amem necesse est
et Veraniolum meum et Fabullum.

ROBERT HERRICK (1591-1674)

Upon Shark. Epigram

SHARK when he goes to any publick feast,
Eates to ones thinking, of all there, the least.
What saves the master of the House thereby?
When if the servants search, they may descry
In his wide Codpeece, (dinner being done)
Two Napkins cram'd up, and a silver Spoone.

Carmen 13.

Cenabis bene, mi Fabulle, apud me
paucis, si tibi di favent, diebus,
si tecum attuleris bonam atque magnam
cenam, non sine candida puella
et vino et sale et omnibus cachinnis.
Haec si, inquam, attuleris, venuste noster,
cenabis bene: nam tui Catulli
plenus sacculus est aranearum.
Sed contra accipies meros amores
seu quid suavius elegantiusve est.
Nam unguentum dabo quod meae puellae
donarunt Veneres Cupidinesque,
quod tu cum olfacies, deos rogabis
totum ut te faciant, Fabulle, nasum.

BEN JONSON (1573?-1637)

Cynthia's Revels, V, 2

Perfumer (*to Amorphus*) "Taste, smell; I assure you, sir, pure benjamin, the only spirited scent that ever awaked a Neapolitan nostril. You would wish yourself all nose for the love on't."

ROBERT HERRICK (1591-1674)

From *Againe*

When I thy singing next shall heare,
Ile wish I might turne all to eare,
To drink in Notes, and Numbers;—

From *To live merrily, and to trust to Good Verses*

A Goblet next Ile drink
  To *Ovid*; and suppose,
Made he the pledge, he'd think
  The world had all *one Nose*.

Then this immensive cup
  Of *Aromatike* wine,
Catullus, I quaffe up
  To that Terce Muse of thine.

Carmen 16.

Pedicabo ego vos et inrumabo,
Aureli pathice et cinaede Furi,
qui me ex versiculis meis putastis,
quod sunt molliculi, parum pudicum.
Nam castum esse decet pium poetam
ipsum, versiculos nihil necesse est,
qui tum denique habent salem ac leporem,
si sunt molliculi ac parum pudici
et quod pruriat incitare possunt,
non dico pueris, sed his pilosis
qui duros nequeunt movere lumbos.
Vos, qui milia multa basiorum
legistis, male me marem putatis?
Pedicabo ego vos et inrumabo.

ROBERT HERRICK (1591-1674)

Last lines of the *Hesperides*

To his Book's end this last line he'd have plac't,
Jocond his Muse was; but his Life was chast.

A request to the Graces

Ponder my words, if so that any be
Known guilty here of incivility:
Let what is graceless, discompos'd, and rude,
With sweetness, smoothness, softness, be endu'd.
Teach it to blush, to curtsie, lisp, and shew
Demure, but yet, full of temptation too.
Numbers ne'r tickle, or but lightly please,
Unlesse they have some wanton carriages.
This if ye do, each Piece will here be good,
And gracefull made, by your neate Sisterhood.

J. C. SQUIRE (*The Living Age*, April 28, 1923)

To A Roman

I

You died two thousand years ago, Catullus,
Myriads since then have walked the earth you knew
All their long lives and faded into nothing,
And still across that waste men think of you.

You loved your Sirmio, and loved your brother,
You gave a pitiless woman all your heart;
You wrote for her, you mourned a sparrow for her,
Served like a slave: and suffering made your art.

Some fiery songs, a few soft elegies,
Perfect—you said you used a pumice stone:
Coarse little squibs, a rosy song for a wedding,
What else you did, it never will be known.

A proud young man of fashion, whom a woman
Played with and dropped: nothing remains beside;
Only we know, about a certain year,
You went away, out of the glare, and died.

And all your world died after, all the towers
Fell, and the temples mouldered, and the games
Left the great circus empty, and the dust
Buried the Caesars, senators, and dames.

II

I see you lying under marble arches,
Above the bright blue meadow of a bay,
With certain supercilious gross companions
Taking their filth more cleverly than they.

Amusing them, one of them, seeming with them:
They are pleased to find Catullus of their kind,
They sprawl and drink and sneer and jest of wenches,
Pose to you: but they do not hear your mind.

You share debauch, debauch does not distract you;
Your wine is tasteless, pleasureless your ease;
Behind your brutal talk you are cold and lonely,
Sick of the laughter of such men as these.

And even they at times perceive you moody,
Bid you cheer up, are vaguely tired of you,
Damper of pleasure, hypocrite, prig, superior,
Too cranky and vain to think as others do.

For suddenly, your answers grow abstracted,
Empty, or rough; your eyes go over sea,
Watching a distant sail that seems unmoving,
The symbol of some lost tranquillity.

A silent sail that cuts the clear horizon,
  A warm blue sea, a tranquil, cloudless sky,
You sit and gaze, and, as you stare, they guess you
  Indifferent though the whole of them should die.

III

"The poet should be chaste, his verses—" Well,
  It wasn't Lesbia's view, she did her best,
Tempting and spurning, to weary and degrade you,
  To callous you and make you like the rest.

Disliking, piqued by, that strange difference in you,
  Contemptuous and curious, she would dare
And then deny, provoke, and then repel you,
  Yet could not make you other than you were.

The soft-pressed foot, the glance that hinted heat,
  The scanty favors always auguring more,
The haughty, cold indifference, mingling twin
  Frigidities of the vestal and the whore,

Still could not even more than wound, cloud over,
  The eager boy in you she so despised,
The love of fineness, sweetness, loyalty, candor,
  The innocent country memories you prized.

IV

A flower in a garden grew, Catullus,
  Sometime you saw it, and the memory stayed.
One flower of all the flowers you ever glanced at,
  A perfect thing of dew and radiance made:

Emblem of youth, plucked, carried away and drooping,
  Out of the garden; emblem of your lot,
Perplexed, bewildered, languishing, an alien
  Who was born to cherish all his world forgot.

Carmen 17.

O Colonia, quae cupis ponte ludere longo,
et salire paratum habes (sed vereris inepta
crura ponticuli assulis stantis in redivivis,
ne supinus eat cavaque in palude recumbat),
sic tibi bonus ex tua pons libidine fiat
in quo vel Salisubsili sacra suscipiantur,
munus hoc mihi maximi da, Colonia, risus.
Quendam municipem meum de tuo volo ponte
ire praecipitem in lutum per caputque pedesque,
verum totius ut lacus putidaeque paludis,
lividissima maximeque est profunda vorago.
Insulsissimus est homo, nec sapit pueri instar
bimuli tremula patris dormientis in ulna.
Cui cum sit viridissimo nupta flore puella
(et puella tenellulo delicatior haedo,
adservanda nigerrimis diligentius uvis),
ludere hanc sinit ut libet, nec pili facit uni,
nec se sublevat ex sua parte, sed velut alnus
in fossa Liguri iacet suppernata securi,
tantundem omnia sentiens quam si nulla sit usquam,
talis iste meus stupor nil videt, nihil audit;
ipse qui sit, utrum sit an non sit, id quoque nescit.
Nunc eum volo de tuo ponte mittere pronum,
si pote stupidum repente excitare veternum
et supinum animum in gravi derelinquere caeno,
ferream ut soleam tenaci in voragine mula.

R. KENNARD DAVIS, *Translations from Catullus*, 1913

O COLONY, that covetest
 a bridge whereon to play,
And art all agog for dancing,
 did a dread not bid you stay,
Lest the rotten legs that carry
 putrid pier and palsied plank
Should swift subside and lodge you
 in the water rich and rank,
May the pretty bridge you pray for
 soon be yours by lucky chance,
One sufficiently substantial
 e'en for Dervishes to dance,
If you will but recompense me
 with a spectacle of mirth,
The fullest and the finest
 and the funniest on earth.
I've a certain fellow townsman—
 I should love to see him go
From your bridge into the water
 to be soused from top to toe,
Just where the muddy moisture
 of your murky, marshy mere
Is dirtiest and deepest
 and most dark and dank and drear!
The man's a perfect simpleton,
 who hasn't got the wit
Of a babe that sleeps serenely
 while its daddy dandles it.
He has married with a maiden
 in her beauty's earliest Spring,
As tender as a lambkin
 by its mother gambolling,
To be guarded as the clusters
 of the ripening grapes and rare,
Yet he lets her flirt at random,
 and he never turns a hair!
He never moves a muscle;
 he lies unheeding, like

An alder by the woodmen felled
    in some Ligurian dyke;
A stock that's quite insensible,
    as blind to what takes place
As it nor there nor anywhere
    were occupying space!
Such is my prince of boobies:
    he can neither see nor hear!
E'en of his own existence
    he scarcely seems aware!
But now I wish to see him
    plunge, from your piers propelled;
Perchance the sudden sousing
    might stir the sloth of eld,
And, as in clinging quicksands
    a mule's cast shoe adheres,
So might your mudbanks bury
    the indolence of years.

Carmen 21. (lines 1-8)

Aureli, pater esuritionum,
non harum modo sed quot aut fuerunt
aut sunt aut aliis erunt in annis,
pedicare cupis meos amores.
Nec clam: nam simul es, iocaris una,
haerens ad latus omnia experiris.
Frustra: nam insidias mihi instruentem
tangam te prior inrumatione.
. . . .

BEN JONSON (1573?-1637)

The Alchemist, 1, 1

Face But I shall put you in mind, sir; at Pie-corner,
Taking your meal of steam in, from cooks' stalls,
Where, like the father of hunger, you did walk
Piteously costive . . .

WALTER SAVAGE LANDOR (1775-1864)

From *Poems and Epigrams*

Aurelius, Sire of Hungrinesses!
Thee thy old friend Catullus blesses,
And sends thee six fine watercresses.
There are who would not think me quite
(Unless we were old friends) polite
To mention whom you should invite.
Look at them well; and turn it o'er
In your own mind—I'd have but four,
Lucullus, Caesar, and two more.

Carmen 22.

Suffenus iste, Vare, quem probe nosti,
homo est venustus et dicax et urbanus,
idemque longe plurimos facit versus.
Puto esse ego illi milia aut decem aut plura
perscripta, nec sic, ut fit, in palimpseston
relata: chartae regiae, novi libri,
novi umbilici, lora rubra membranae,
derecta plumbo et pumice omnia aequata.
Haec cum legas tu, bellus ille et urbanus
Suffenus unus caprimulgus aut fossor
rursus videtur: tantum abhorret ac mutat.
Hoc quid putemus esse? Qui modo scurra
aut si quid hac re tritius videbatur,
idem infaceto est infacetior rure
simul poemata attigit, neque idem umquam
aeque est beatus ac poema cum scribit:
tam gaudet in se tamque se ipse miratur.
Nimirum idem omnes fallimur, neque est quisquam
quem non in aliqua re videre Suffenum
possis. Suus cuique attributus est error
sed non videmus manticae quod in tergo est.

Thomas Campion (1567?-1619)

From *Epigrammatum Liber Secundus*

Cum tibi vilescat doctus lepidusque Catullus;
Non est ut sperem, Cambre, placere tibi.
Tu quoque cum Suffenorum suffragia quaeras;
Non est ut speres, Cambre, placere mihi.

Robert Herrick (1591-1674)

Upon Pievish. Epigram

PIEVISH doth boast, that he's the very first
Of English Poets, and 'tis thought the Worst.

Our own sinnes unseen

Other mens sins wee ever beare in mind;
None sees the fardell of his faults behind.

John Marston (1575?-1634)

From *The Scourge of Villainy, Satire* XI, 178ff

But O, Suffenus! (that doth hug, embrace
His proper self, admire his own sweet face;
Praiseth his own fair limbs' proportion,
Kisseth his shade, recounteth all alone
His own good parts) who envies him? Not I,
For well he may, without all rivalry.

Samuel Rowlands (c. 1570-1630)

From the *Satires*

Derision hath an ore in everie Boate,
In's Neighboures eie he quickly spies a moate,
But the great beame that's noted in his owne,
He lets remaine, and never thinkes thereon.
Some do report he beares about a sacke,
Halfe hanging forwards, halfe behind at's backe:
And his owne faultes (quite out of sight and minde)
He casts into the part that hanges behinde:
But other mens he putteth in before,
And into them he looketh evermore.

Carmen 23.

Furi, cui neque servus est neque arca
nec cimex neque araneus neque ignis,
verum est et pater et noverca quorum
dentes vel silicem comesse possunt,
est pulchre tibi cum tuo parente
et cum coniuge lignea parentis.
Nec mirum: bene nam valetis omnes,
pulchre concoquitis, nihil timetis,
non incendia, non graves ruinas,
non facta impia, non dolos veneni,
non casus alios periculorum.
Atqui corpora sicciora cornu
aut si quid magis aridum est habetis
sole et frigore et esuritione.
Quare non tibi sit bene ac beate?
. . . .
Haec tu commoda tam beata, Furi,
noli spernere nec putare parvi;
et sestertia quae soles precari
centum desine: nam sat es beatus.

FRANKLIN P. ADAMS, *Weights and Measures*, 1917

To Furius, on Poverty

Financial troubles irk thee not;
No servants test thy strong endurance;
No germs infest thy simple cot;
Thou hast no need for fire insurance.

How happy, Furius, is thy life
Shared with thine estimable Popper
And his—excuse me—wooden wife!
(I think those birds could lunch on copper!)

In utter health how happy thou,
Fearing nor fire nor indigestion!
No fall in stocks can blanch thy brow
Serene beyond all doubt or question.

Hay fever, rheumatiz, the grip,
Malaria, gout, and such diseases
Elude thy frugal guardianship—
Both when it's hot and when it freezes.

Cease then to pray the gods for wealth
Not worth the pains to have amassed it!
I wonder if, with naught but health
Thou knowest just how soft thou hast it?

Carmen 29 (lines 1-10)

Quis hoc potest videre, quis potest pati,
nisi impudicus et vorax et aleo,
Mamurram habere quod Comata Gallia
habebat ante et ultima Britannia?
Cinaede Romule, haec videbis et feres?
Et ille nunc superbus et superfluens
perambulabit omnium cubilia
aut albulus columbus aut Adoneus?
Cinaede Romule, haec videbis et feres?
Es impudicus et vorax et aleo.
. . . .

GEORGE GORDON BYRON, LORD BYRON (1788-1824)

From *To Thomas Moore*

Written the evening before his visit to Mr. Leigh Hunt in Horsemonger Lane Gaol; dated May 19, 1813.

But now to my letter—to *yours* 'tis an answer—
Tomorrow be with me, as soon as you can, Sir,
All ready and dressed for proceeding to spunge on
(According to compact) the wit in the dungeon—
Pray Phoebus at length our political malice
May not get us lodgings within the same palace!
I suppose that to-night you're engaged with some codgers,
And for Sotheby's Blues have deserted Sam Rogers;
And I, though with cold I have nearly my death got,
Must put on my breeches, and wait on the Heathcote;
But to-morrow, at four, we will both play the *Scurra*,
And you'll be Catullus, the Regent, Mamurra. Mamurra.

Carmen 31.

Paene insularum, Sirmio, insularumque
ocelle quascumque in liquentibus stagnis
marique vasto fert uterque Neptunus,
quam te libenter quamque laetus inviso,
vix mi ipse credens Thyniam atque Bithynos
liquisse campos et videre te in tuto.
O quid solutis est beatius curis,
cum mens onus reponit ac peregrino
labore fessi venimus Larem ad nostrum
desideratoque adquiescimus lecto!
Hoc est quod unum est pro laboribus tantis
Salve, o venusta Sirmio, atque ero gaude;
gaudete vosque, o Lydiae lacus undae;
ridete, quidquid est domi cachinnorum.

William Shakespeare (1564-1616)

From *Sonnet* XXVII

Weary with toil, I haste me to my bed,
The dear repose for limbs with travel tired;

Walter Savage Landor (1775-1864)

On Catullus

Tell me not what too well I know
About the bard of Sirmio . . . .
    Yes, in Thalia's son
Such stains there are—as when a Grace
Sprinkles another's laughing face
    With nectar, and runs on.

Alfred Tennyson (1809-1892)

"Frater Ave Atque Vale"

Row us out from Desenzano, to your Sirmione row!
So they row'd, and there we landed—"O venusta Sirmio!"
There to me thro' all the groves of olive in the summer glow,
There beneath the Roman ruin where the purple flowers grow,
Came that "Ave atque Vale" of the Poet's hopeless woe,
Tenderest of Roman poets nineteen hundred years ago,
"Frater Ave atque Vale," as we wander'd to and fro,
Gazing at the Lydian laughter of the Garda Lake below,
Sweet Catullus's all-but-island, olive-silvery Sirmio!

Charles Stuart Calverley, *Verses and Translations*, 1862

Gem of all isthmuses and isles that lie,
    Fresh or salt water's children, in clear lake
Or ampler ocean: with what joy do I
    Approach thee, Sirmio! Oh! am I awake,
Or dream that once again mine eye beholds
Thee, and has looked its last on Thracian wolds?
    Sweetest of sweets to me that pastime seems,
When the mind drops her burden: when—the pain
Of travel past—our own cot we regain,

And nestle on the pillow of our dreams!
'Tis this one thought that cheers us as we roam.
Hail, O fair Sirmio! Joy, thy lord is here!
Joy too, ye waters of the Golden Mere!
And ring out, all ye laughter-peals of home!

ALGERNON CHARLES SWINBURNE (1837-1909)

From "*Insularum Ocelle*"

Sark, fairer than aught in the world that the lit skies cover,
Laughs inly behind her cliffs, and the seafarers mark
As a shrine where the sunlight serves, though the blown clouds hover,
Sark.

We mourn, for love of a song that outsang the lark,
That nought so lovely beholden of Sirmio's lover
Made glad in Propontis the flight of his Pontic bark.

From *Song for the Centenary of Walter Savage Landor*

With gracious gods he communed, honouring thus
At once by service and similitude,
Service devout and worship emulous
Of the same golden Muses once they wooed,
The names and shades adored of all of us,
The nurslings of the brave world's earlier brood,
Grown gods for us themselves: Theocritus
First, and more dear Catullus, names bedewed
With blessings bright like tears
From the old memorial years,
And loves and lovely laughters, every mood
Sweet as the drops that fell
Of their own oenomel
From living lips to cheer the multitude
That feeds on words divine, and grows
More worthy, seeing their world reblossom like a rose.

THOMAS HARDY, (After passing Sirmione,) April 1887.

Sirmio, thou dearest dear of strands
That Neptune strokes in lake and sea,
With what high joy from stranger lands
Doth thy old friend set foot on thee!
Yea, barely seems it true to me
That no Bithynia holds me now,
But calmly and assuringly
Around me stretchest homely Thou.
Is there a scene more sweet than when
Our clinging cares are undercast,
And, worn by alien moils and men,
The long untrodden sill repassed,
We press the kindly couch at last,
And find a full repayment there?
Then hail, sweet Sirmio; thou that wast,
And art, mine own unrivalled Fair!

LAURENCE BINYON, *England and other Poems*, 1909

Sirmione[1]

Give me thy hand, Belov'd! I cannot see;
So close above our steps, from tree to tree,
Shadows hang over us. How huge and still
Night sleeps! and yet a murmur, a low thrill,
Sighed out of mystery, steals slowly near,
Solitary as longing or as fear,
Through the faint foliage, stirring it, and shy
Amid the stillness, ere it tremble by,
Touches us on the cheek and on the brow
Light as a dew-dipt finger! Listen now,
'Tis not alone the hushings of the bough,
But on the slabbed rack-beaches far beneath,
Listen, the liquid breath
Of the vast lake that rustles up all round
Whispering for ever! Soon shall we be where
The trees end, and the promontory bare

[1] Reprinted in *Selected Poems of Laurence Binyon.* Copyright (1922) by The Macmillan Company. Reprinted here by permission.

Breathes all that wide and water-wandering air
Which shall our foreheads and our lips delight,
Blown darkly through the breadth and depth and height
Of soft, immense, and solitary Night.

—Where is the Day,
Bright as a dream, that on this same cliff-way
Fretted light shadows on old olive stems,
By whose gray, riven roots, like scarlet gems,
The little poppies burned? Where those clear hues
Of water, melted to diviner blues
In the deep distance of each radiant bay,
But close beneath us, past the narrowed edge
Of shadow from sheer crag and jutting ledge,
Shallowing upon the low reef into gold,
A ripple of keen light for ever rolled
Up to the frail reed sighing on the shore?
Where are those mountains far-enthroned and hoar
Above the glittering water's slumbrous heat,
With old blanched towns sprinkled about their feet,
Lifting majestic shoulders, that each side
Of that steep misty northern chasm divide,
Where, ambushed in the dim gulf ere they leap,
Wild spirits of the Wind and Thunder sleep?
'Tis flown, that many-coloured dream is flown,
And with the heart of Night we are alone.

This is the verge. The promontory ends.
Now the soft branches cover us no more.
Abrupt the path descends:
But we will sit here, high upon the shore,
Here, where we know what wild flowered bushes cloak
Old ruined walls, and crumbling arches choke
With mounded earth, though buried from our eyes
In dark now, as beneath dark centuries
That marble-towered magnificence of Rome,
From whose hot dust the passionate poet fled
Hither, and laid his head
Where these same waters laughed him welcome home.

It is all dark; but how the air breathes free!
Beloved, lean to me!
Feel how the stillness like a bath desired
With happy pressure heals our senses tired;
And drink the keen sweet fragrance from the grass
And wafts from hidden flowers that come and pass,—
None here but we, and we have left behind
Noise of the rough world, in its cares confined,
All with the daylight drowned
In darkness on this height of utmost ground,
Where under us the sighing waters cease
And over us are only stars and peace.

Carmen 35.

Poetae tenero, meo sodali
velim Caecilio, papyre, dicas
Veronam veniat, Novi relinquens
Comi moenia Lariumque litus:
nam quasdam volo cogitationes
amici accipiat sui meique.
Quare, si sapiet, viam vorabit,
quamvis candida milies puella
euntem revocet manusque collo
ambas iniciens roget morari,
quae nunc, si mihi vera nuntiantur,
illum deperit impotente amore:
nam quo tempore legit incohatam
DINDYMI DOMINAM, ex eo misellae
ignes interiorem edunt medullam.
Ignosco tibi, Sapphica puella
Musa doctior: est enim venuste
MAGNA Caecilio incohata MATER.

Pilgrimage to Parnassus; Comedy performed in S. John's College, Cambridge, Dec. 1597.

Act I, 96ff.

Associate yourselvs with studious youthes,
That, as Catullus saith, devoure the waye
That leads to Parnassus where content doth dwell.

BEN JONSON (1573?-1637)

Sejanus, V, 10

They greedily devour the way
To some great sports.

JONATHAN SWIFT (1667-1745)

From *Cadenus and Vanessa*

Cadenus many things had writ:
Vanessa much esteemed his wit,
And called for his poetic works:
Meantime the boy in secret lurks,
And, while the book was in her hand,
The urchin from his private stand
Took aim, and shot with all his strength
A dart of such prodigious length,
It pierced the feeble volume through,
And deep transfixed her bosom too.
Some lines, more moving than the rest,
Stuck to the point that pierced her breast,
And, borne directly to the heart,
With pains unknown increased her smart.

Carmen 38.

Male est, Cornifici, tuo Catullo;
male est me hercule et laboriose,
et magis magis in dies et horas.
Quem tu, quod minimum facillimumque est,
qua solatus es adlocutione?
Irascor tibi. Sic meos amores?
Paulum quid libet adlocutionis,
maestius lacrimis Simonideis.

LEIGH HUNT (1784-1859)

Sick, Cornificius, is thy friend,
Sick to the heart: and sees no end
Of wretched thoughts that gathering fast
Threaten to wear him out at last.

And yet you never come and bring,
Though 'twere the least and easiest thing,
A comfort in that talk of thine.
You vex me. This to love of mine?

Prithee a little talk, for ease,
Full as the tears of sad Simonides!

Carmen 44.

O funde noster seu Sabine seu Tiburs,
(nam te esse Tiburtem autumant, quibus non est
cordi Catullum laedere; at quibus cordi est,
quovis Sabinum pignore esse contendunt)
sed seu Sabine sive verius Tiburs,
fui libenter in tua suburbana
villa malamque pectore exspui tussim,
non immerenti quam mihi meus venter,
dum sumptuosas appeto, dedit, cenas:
nam, Sestianus dum volo esse conviva,
orationem in Antium petitorem
plenam veneni et pestilentiae legi.
Hic me gravedo frigida et frequens tussis
quassavit usque, dum in tuum sinum fugi
et me recuravi otioque et urtica.
Quare refectus maximas tibi grates
ago, meum quod non es ulta peccatum.
Nec deprecor iam, si nefaria scripta
Sesti recepso, quin gravedinem et tussim
non mihi, sed ipsi Sestio ferat frigus,
qui tunc vocat me, cum malum librum legi.

JONATHAN SWIFT (1667-1745)

On burning a dull poem, 1729

An ass's hoof alone can hold
That poisonous juice which kills by cold
Methought when I this poem read,
No vessel but an ass's head
Such frigid fustian could contain;
I mean, the head without the brain.
The cold conceits, the chilling thoughts,
Went down like stupefying draughts;
I found my head began to swim,
A numbness crept through every limb.
In haste with imprecations dire,
I threw the volume in the fire;
When (who could think?) though cold as ice,
It burnt to ashes in a trice.
How could I more enhance its fame?
Though born in snow, it died in flame.

Carmen 45.

Acmen Septimius suos amores
tenens in gremio, "Mea," inquit, "Acme,
ni te perdite amo atque amare porro
omnes sum assidue paratus annos
quantum qui pote plurimum perire,
solus in Libya Indiaque tosta
caesio veniam obvius leoni."
Hoc ut dixit, Amor sinistra ut ante,
dextra sternuit approbationem.
At Acme leviter caput reflectens
et dulcis pueri ebrios ocellos
illo purpureo ore saviata,
"Sic," inquit, "mea vita Septimille,
huic uni domino usque serviamus,
ut multo mihi maior acriorque
ignis mollibus ardet in medullis."
Hoc ut dixit, Amor sinistra ut ante,
dextra sternuit approbationem.
Nunc ab auspicio bono profecti
mutuis animis amant, amantur.
Unam Septimius misellus Acmen
mavult quam Syrias Britanniasque;
uno in Septimio fidelis Acme
facit delicias libidinesque.
Quis ullos homines beatiores
vidit, quis Venerem auspicatiorem?

ABRAHAM COWLEY (1618-1667)

Acme and Septimius

Whilst on Septimius panting Breast
(Meaning nothing less than Rest)
Acme lean'd her loving Head,
Thus the pleas'd Septimius said:

My dearest *Acme*, if I be
Once alive, and love not thee,
With a Passion far above
All that e'er was called Love,
In a *Lybian* Desert may
I become some Lion's Prey;
Let him, *Acme*, let him tear
My Breast—when *Acme* is not there.

The God of Love, who stood to hear him,
(The God of Love was always near him)
Pleas'd and tickl'd with the Sound,
Sneez'd aloud; and all around
The little Loves, that waited by,
Bow'd, and bless'd the Augury.

Acme, enflam'd with what he said,
Rear'd her gently-bending Head,
And her purple Mouth with Joy,
Stretching to the delicious Boy,
Twice (and twice could scarce suffice)
She kiss'd his drunken, rolling Eyes.

"My little Life, my All (said she)
So may we ever Servants be
To this best God, and ne'er retain
Our hated Liberty again;
So may thy Passion last for me,
As I a Passion have for thee,
Greater and fiercer much than can

Be conceiv'd by thee, a Man.
Into my Marrow is it gone,
Fix'd and settled in the Bone,
It reigns not only in my Heart,
But runs, like Life, through ev'ry Part.

She spoke; the God of Love aloud
Sneez'd again, and all the Crowd
Of little Loves, that waited by,
Bow'd, and bless'd the Augury.

This good Omen, thus from Heav'n,
Like a happy Signal giv'n,
Their Loves and Lives (all four) embrace,
And Hand in Hand run all the Race.
To poor Septimius (who did now
Nothing else but Acme grow)
Acme's Bosom was alone,
The whole World's Imperial Throne,
And to faithful *Acme's* Mind
Septimius was all Human kind.

If the Gods would please to be
But advis'd for once by me,
I'd advise 'em, when they spy
Any illustrious Piety,
To reward her, if it be she,
To reward him, if it be he,
With such a husband, such a wife,
With Acme's and Septimius' Life.

GEORGE GRANVILLE, LORD LANSDOWN (1667-1735)

To Lady Mary Villiers

If I not love thee, Villiers, more
Than ever mortal loved before;
With such a passion, fix'd and sure,
As e'en possession could not cure,
Never to cease but with my breath,
May then this bumper be my death.

GEORGE ELLIS, *Poetry of the Anti-Jacobin*, No. XIII

Acme and Septimius
or,
The Happy Union

Celebrated at the Crown and Anchor Tavern.
February 5, 1798.

FOX, with Tooke to grace his side,
Thus addressed his blooming bride—
"Sweet! should I e'er, in power or place,
Another citizen embrace;
Should e'er my eyes delight to look
On aught alive, save John Horne Tooke,
Doom me to ridicule and ruin,
In the coarse hug of Indian Bruin!"

He spoke; and to the left and right,
Norfolk hiccupped with delight.

Tooke, his bald head gently moving,
On the sweet patriot's drunken eyes
His wine-empurpled lips applies,
And thus returns in accents loving:
"So, my dear Charley, may success
At length my ardent wishes bless,
And lead, through discord's lowering storm,
To one grand *radical reform*!
As, from this hour I love thee more
Than e'er I hated thee before!"

He spoke; and to the left and right,
Norfolk hiccupped with delight.

With this good omen they proceed;
Fond toasts their mutual passion feed;
In Fox's breast Horne Tooke prevails
Before rich Ireland and South Wales;
And Fox (un-read each other book),
Is law and gospel to Horne Tooke.

When were such kindred souls united!
Or wedded pair so much delighted?

ALFRED TENNYSON (1809-1892)

From *Edwin Morris*

Shall not Love to me,
As in the Latin song I learnt at school,
Sneeze out a full God-bless-you right and left?

Carmen 46.

Iam ver egelidos refert tepores,
iam caeli furor aequinoctialis
iucundis Zephyri silescit auris.
Linquantur Phrygii, Catulle, campi
Nicaeaeque ager uber aestuosae;
ad claras Asiae volemus urbes.
Iam mens praetrepidans avet vagari,
iam laeti studio pedes vigescunt.
O dulces comitum valete coetus,
longe quos simul a domo profectos
diversae variae viae reportant.

THOMAS MOORE (1779-1852)

From *Poems relating to America*

And then, that Hope, that fairy Hope,—
  Oh! she awak'd such happy dreams,
And gave my soul such tempting scope
  For all its dearest, fondest schemes,
That not Verona's child of song,
  When flying from the Phrygian shore,
With lighter heart could bound along,
  Or pant to be a wanderer more!

Carmen 48.

Mellitos oculos tuos, Iuventi,
si quis me sinat usque basiare,
usque ad milia basiem trecenta,
nec umquam videar satur futurus,
non si densior aridis aristis
sit nostrae seges osculationis.

Richard Lovelace (1618-1658)

Juvencius, thy fair sweet eyes
If to my fill that I may kisse,
Three hundred thousand times I'de kisse,
Nor future age should cloy this blisse;
No, not if thicker than ripe ears
The harvest of our kisses bears.

Arthur Symons, *Knave of Hearts* (1894-1908)

Your honeyed eyes, Juventius,
If you would let one kiss,
Three hundred thousand would to us
Seem nothing much amiss:
Could all earth's ears of corn eclipse
That heavenly harvest of the lips?

Carmen 49.

Disertissime Romuli nepotum,
quot sunt quotque fuere, Marce Tulli,
quotque post aliis erunt in annis,
gratias tibi maximas Catullus
agit pessimus omnium poeta,
tanto pessimus omnium poeta
quanto tu optimus omnium patronus.

CHRISTOPHER SMART (1722-1771)

(Imitated after Dining with Mr. Murray)

O Thou, of British orators the chief
That were, or are in being, or belief;
All eminence and goodness as thou art,
Accept the gratitude of Poet Smart,—
The meanest of the tuneful train as far,
As thou transcend'st the brightest at the bar.

Carmen 50.

Hesterno, Licini, die otiosi
multum lusimus in meis tabellis,
ut convenerat esse delicatos.
Scribens versiculos uterque nostrum
ludebat numero modo hoc modo illoc,
reddens mutua per iocum atque vinum.
Atque illinc abii tuo lepore
incensus, Licini, facetiisque,
ut nec me miserum cibus iuvaret
nec somnus tegeret quiete ocellos,
sed toto indomitus furore lecto
versarer cupiens videre lucem,
ut tecum loquerer simulque ut essem.
At defessa labore membra postquam
semimortua lectulo iacebant,
hoc, iucunde, tibi poema feci,
ex quo perspiceres meum dolorem.
Nunc audax cave sis precesque nostras,
oramus, cave despuas, ocelle,
ne poenas Nemesis reposcat a te.
Est vehemens dea: laedere hanc caveto.

From *The Adventures of Catullus, and History of his Amours with Lesbia.*

Intermixt with Translations of his Choicest Poems. By several Hands. Done from the French. London, 1707.

Licinius, yesterday at Leisure
We in my tablets took much pleasure,
As either of us then thought fit
To Versify, and deal in Wit;
Now in this sort of Verse, now that,
As Mirth and Wine indulg'd the Chat.
And thence *Licinius* did I part,
So griev'd with thy Replies so smart,
That ev'n my Food deny'd me Ease,
Nor could Sleep my Eye-Lids seize:
But tumbling in my Bed all Night,
I coveted to see the Light,
That with *Licinius* I may be,
And in Discourse again be free.
But when my Limbs with Toil oppress'd,
Half dead, half seem'd to take their rest,
This I my merry Comrade sent,
That you might know my Discontent.
Take care now, be not Proud and High,
Nor slight my Prayers with haughty Eye,
Lest *Nemesis* Reprizals make,
And of thy Pride just Vengeance take;
For she's a Goddess, oh! take care
How you provoke her: will not spare.

Carmen 51.

Ille mi par esse deo videtur,
ille, si fas est, superare divos,
qui sedens adversus identidem te
spectat et audit

dulce ridentem, misero quod omnis
eripit sensus mihi: nam simul te,
Lesbia, adspexi, nihil est super mi
. . . .
lingua sed torpet, tenuis sub artus
flamma demanat, sonitu suopte
tintinant aures, gemina teguntur
lumina nocte.

Otium, Catulle, tibi molestum est;
otio exsultas nimiumque gestis;
otium et reges prius et beatas
perdidit urbes.

Percy Bysshe Shelley (1792-1822)

To Constantia Singing

My brain is wild, my breath comes quick,—
  The blood is listening in my frame,
And thronging shadows, fast and thick,
  Fall on my overflowing eyes:
My heart is quivering like a flame;
As morning dew, that in the sunbeam dies,
I am dissolved in these consuming ecstasies.

Alfred Tennyson (1809-1892)

From *Eleänore*

    I watch thy grace; and in its place
My heart a charmed slumber keeps,
    While I muse upon thy face;
And a languid fire creeps
    Thro' my veins to all my frame,
Dissolvingly and slowly: soon
    From thy rose-red lips MY name
 Floweth; and then, as in a swoon,
  With dinning sound my ears are rife,
    My tremulous tongue faltereth,
  I lose my colour, I lose my breath,
  I drink the cup of a costly death,
Brimm'd with delirious draughts of warmest life.

William Ewart Gladstone (1809-1898)

Him rival to the gods I place,
  Him loftier yet, if loftier be,
Who, Lesbia, sits before thy face,
  Who listens and who looks on thee;

Thee smiling soft. Yet this delight
    Doth all my sense consign to death;
For when thou dawnest on my sight,
    Ah, wretched! flits my labouring breath.

My tongue is palsied. Subtly hid
    Fire creeps me through from limb to limb:
My loud ears tingle all unbid:
    Twin clouds of night mine eyes bedim.

Ease is my plague: ease makes thee void,
    Catullus, with these vacant hours,
And wanton: ease that hath destroyed
    Great kings, and states with all their powers.

Carmen 61.

Collis o Heliconii
cultor, Uraniae genus,
qui rapis teneram ad virum
virginem, o Hymenaee Hymen,
o Hymen Hymenaee,

cinge tempora floribus
suave olentis amaraci,
flammeum cape laetus, huc
huc veni, niveo gerens
luteum pede soccum,

excitusque hilari die,
nuptialia concinens
voce carmina tinnula,
pelle humum pedibus, manu
pineam quate taedam.

Namque Iunia Manlio,
qualis Idalium colens
venit ad Phrygium Venus
iudicem, bona cum bona
nubet alite virgo,

floridis velut enitens
myrtus Asia ramulis,
quos Hamadryades deae
ludicrum sibi rosido
nutriunt umore.

Quare age huc aditum ferens
perge linquere Thespiae
rupis Aonios specus,
nympha quos super inrigat
frigerans Aganippe;

EDMUND SPENSER (1552?-1599)

From the *Epithalamion*

Bid her awake; for Hymen is awake,
And long since ready forth his maske to move,
With his bright Tead that flames with many a flake,
And many a bachelor to waite on him,
In theyr fresh garments trim.

. . . .

Now is my love all ready forth to come:
Let all the virgins therefore well awayt:
And ye fresh boyes, that tend upon her groome,
Prepare your selves; for he is comming strayt.
Set all your things in seemely good aray,
Fit for so joyfull day:
The joyfulst day that ever sunne did see.

. . . .

But, most of all, the Damzels doe delite
When they their tymbrels smyte,
And thereunto doe daunce and carrol sweet,
That all the sences they doe ravish quite;
The whyles the boyes run up and downe the street,
Crying aloud with strong confused noyce,
As if it were one voyce,
Hymen, iö Hymen, Hymen, they do shout;
That even to the heavens theyr shouting shrill
Doth reach, and all the firmament doth fill;
To which the people standing all about,
As in approvance, doe thereto applaud,
And loud advaunce her laud;
And evermore they Hymen, Hymen sing,
That al the woods them answer, and theyr eccho ring.

. . . .

Open the temple gates unto my love,
Open them wide that she may enter in,
And all the postes adorne as doth behove,
And all the pillours deck with girlands trim,
For to receyve this Saynt with honour dew,
That commeth in to you.

. . . .

Carmen 61.

ac domum dominam voca
coniugis cupidam novi,
mentem amore revinciens,
ut tenax hedera huc et huc
    arborem implicat errans.

Vosque item simul, integrae
virgines, quibus advenit
par dies, agite in modum
dicite, "O Hymenaee Hymen,
    o Hymen Hymenaee,"

ut libentius, audiens
se citarier ad suum
munus, huc aditum ferat
dux bonae Veneris, boni
    coniugator amoris.

Quis deus magis anxiis
est petendus amantibus?
Quem colent homines magis
caelitum? O Hymenaee Hymen,
    o Hymen Hymenaee.

Te suis tremulus parens
invocat, tibi virgines
zonula soluunt sinus,
te timens cupida novus
    captat aure maritus.

Tu fero iuveni in manus
floridam ipse puellulam
dedis a gremio suae
matris, o Hymenaee Hymen,
    o Hymen Hymenaee.

Now al is done: bring home the bride againe;
Bring home the triumph of our victory:
Bring home with you the glory of her gaine
With joyance bring her and with jollity.
Never had man more joyfull day then this,
Whom heaven would heape with blis . . .

Ah! when will this long weary day have end,
And lende me leave to come unto my love?
How slowly do the houres theyr numbers spend?
How slowly does sad Time his feathers move?
Hast thee, O fayrest Planet, to thy home,
Within the Westerne fome:
Thy tyred steedes long since have need of rest.
Long though it be, at last I see it gloome,
And the bright evening-star with golden creast
Appeare out of the East.
Fayre childe of beauty! glorious lampe of love!
That all the host of heaven in rankes doost lead,
And guydest lovers through the nights sad dread,
How chearefully thou lookest from above,
And seemst to laugh atweene thy twinkling light,
As joying in the sight
Of these glad many, which for joy doe sing,
That all the woods them answer, and their echo ring!

Now ceasse, ye damsels, your delights fore-past;
Enough it is that all the day was youres:
Now day is doen, and night is nighing fast,
Now bring the Bryde into the brydall boures.
The night is come, now soon her disaray.
And in her bed her lay;
Lay her in lillies and in violets,
And silken courteins over her display,
And odoured sheetes, and Arras coverlets.
Behold how goodly my faire love does ly,
In proud humility!
Like unto Maia, when as Jove her took
In Tempe, lying on the flowry gras,
Twixt sleepe and wake, after she weary was,

Carmen 61.

Nil potest sine te Venus
fama quod bona comprobet
commodi capere, at potest
te volente. Quis huic deo
    compararier ausit?

Nulla quit sine te domus
liberos dare nec parens
stirpe nitier, at potest
te volente. Quis huic deo
    compararier ausit?

Quae tuis careat sacris
non queat dare praesides
terra finibus, at queat
te volente. Quis huic deo
    compararier ausit?

Claustra pandite ianuae:
virgo adest. Viden ut faces
splendidas quatiunt comas?
. . . .
. . . .

. . . .
. . . .
tardet ingenuus pudor;
quem tamen magis audiens
    flet quod ire necesse est.

With bathing in the Acidalian brooke.
Now it is night, ye damsels may be gon,
And leave my love alone,
And leave likewise your former lay to sing:
The woods no more shall answere, nor your echo ring.

. . . .

And thou, great Juno! which with awful might
The lawes of wedlock still dost patronize;
And the religion of the faith first plight
With sacred rites hast taught to solemnize;
And eeke for comfort often called art
Of women in their smart;
Eternally bind thou this lovely band,
And all thy blessings unto us impart.
And thou, glad Genius! in whose gentle hand
The bridale bowre and geniall bed remaine,
Without blemish or staine;
And the sweet pleasures of theyr loves delight
With secret ayde doest succour and supply,
Till they bring forth the fruitfull progeny;
Send us the timely fruit of this same night.
And thou, fayre Hebe! and thou, Hymen free!
Grant that it may so be.
Til which we cease your further prayse to sing;
Ne any woods shall answer, nor your Eccho ring.

WILLIAM SHAKESPEARE (1564-1616)

Comedy of Errors, II, 2, 175ff.

Adriana Come, I will fasten on this sleeve of thine:
Thou art an elm, my husband, I a vine,
Whose weakness married to thy stronger state
Makes me with thy strength to communicate . . .

Midsummer Night's Dream, IV, 1, 46ff.

Titania Sleep thou, and I will wind thee in my arms;
to Fairies, begone, and be all ways away!
Bottom So doth the woodbine the sweet honeysuckle
Gently entwist; the female ivy so
Enrings the barky fingers of the elm.

Flere desine. Non tibi, Au-
runculeia, periculum est
ne qua femina pulchrior
clarum ab Oceano diem
 viderit venientem.

Talis in vario solet
divitis domini hortulo
stare flos hyacinthinus.
Sed moraris, abit dies;
 prodeas, nova nupta.

Prodeas, nova nupta, si
iam videtur, et audias
nostra verba. Vide ut faces
aureas quatiunt comas;
 prodeas, nova nupta.

Non tuus levis in mala
deditus vir adultera
probra turpia persequens
a tuis teneris volet
 secubare papillis,

lenta quin velut adsitas
vitis implicat arbores,
implicabitur in tuum
complexum. Sed abit dies;
 prodeas, nova nupta.

Henry Peacham (1576?-1643?)

Nuptial Hymn in Honour of the Marriage between Frederick, Count Palatine of the Rhine, and the Princess Elizabeth, Daughter of James 1, 1613.

Urania's son, who dwell'st upon
The fertile top of Helicon,
Chaste marriage sovereign, and dost lead
The virgin to her bridal bed:
    Io, Hymen, Hymenaeus!

With marjoram begirt thy brow,
And take the veil of yellow: now
Ye piny torches with your light,
To golden day convert the night:
    Io, Hymen, Hymenaeus!

See how like the Cyprian queen,
Eliza comes, as when (I ween)
On Ida hill the prize she had
Allotted by the Phrygian lad:
    Io, Hymen, Hymenaeus.

As Asian myrtles fresh and fair,
Which Hamadryads with their care,
And duly tending by the floods,
Have taught to over-look the woods:
    Io, Hymen, Hymenaeus!

Behold now Vesper from the sky
Consenteth by his twinkling eye;
And Cynthia stays her swans to see
The state of this solemnity:
    Io, Hymen, Hymenaeus!

Wedlock, were it not for thee,
We could not child or parent see,
Armies, countries to defend,
Or shepherds, hilly herds to tend:
    Io, Hymen, Hymenaeus!

Carmen 61.

O cubile quod omnibus
. . . .
. . . .
. . . .
    candido pede lecti,

quae tuo veniunt ero,
quanta gaudia, quae vaga
nocte, quae medio die
gaudeat. Sed abit dies;
    prodeas, nova nupta.

Tollite, o pueri, faces:
flammeum video venire.
Ite, concinite in modum,
"O Hymen Hymenaee io,
    o Hymen Hymenaee."

Ne diu taceat procax
Fescennina iocatio
nec nuces pueris neget
desertum domini audiens
    concubinus amorem.

Da nuces pueris, iners
concubine: satis diu
lusisti nucibus. Libet
iam servire Talasio.
    Concubine, nuces da.

But, Hymen, call the nymph away,
With torches' light the children stay,
Whose sparks (see how!) ascend on high
As if there wanted stars in sky:
Io, Hymen, Hymenaeus!

As virgin vine her elm doth wed,
His oak the ivy over-spread;
So chaste desires thou join'st in one,
That disunited were undone:
Io, Hymen, Hymenaeus!

But see! her golden foot hath past
The doubled threshold, and at last
She doth approach her bridal-bed
Of none save Tiber envyed:
Io, Hymen, Hymenaeus!

Chaste marriage-bed, he sooner tells
The stars, the ocean sand or shells,
That thinks to number those delights,
Wherewith thou short'nest longest nights:
Io, Hymen, Hymenaeus!

With richest Tyrian purple spread,
Where her dear spouse is laid on bed,
Like young Ascanius, or the lad
Her love the queen of Cyprus had:
Io, Hymen, Hymenaeus!

Young Frederick, of royal line,
Of Cassimires, who on the Rhine
To none are second said to be
For valour, bounty, piety:
Io, Hymen, Hymenaeus!

Come bride-maid Venus, and undo
Th'Herculean knot with fingers two;
And take the girdle from her waist,
That virgins must forego at last:
Io, Hymen, Hymenaeus!

Sordebant tibi vilicae,
concubine, hodie atque heri;
nunc tuum cinerarius
tondet os. Miser a! miser
    concubine, nuces da.

Diceris male te a tuis
unguentate glabris marite
abstinere; sed abstine.
O Hymen Hymenaee io,
 o Hymen Hymenaee.

Scimus haec tibi quae licent
sola cognita; sed marito
ista non eadem licent.
O Hymen Hymenaee io,
    o Hymen Hymenaee.

Nupta, tu quoque, quae tuus
vir petet, cave ne neges,
ne petitum aliunde eat.
O Hymen Hymenaee io,
    o Hymen Hymenaee.

Scatter nuts without the door,
The married is a child no more;
For whoso'er a wife hath wed
Hath other business in his head:
  Io, Hymen, Hymenaeus!

Where pass ye many an happy night,
Until Lucina brings to light
An hopeful prince, who may restore,
In part, the loss we had before:
  Io, Hymen, Hymenaeus!

That one day we may live to see
A Frederick Henry on her knee;
Who mought to Europe give her law,
And keep encroaching Hell in awe:
  Io, Hymen, Hymenaeus!

Upon whose brow may envy read
The reconcile of love and dread;
And in whose rosy cheek we see
His mother's graceful modesty:
  Io, Hymen, Hymenaeus!

But, Muse of mine, we but molest,
I doubt, with ruder song their rest:
The doors are shut, and lights about
Extinct; then time thy flame were out:
  Io, Hymen, Hymenaeus!

ROBERT HERRICK (1591-1674)

An Epithalamie to Sir Thomas Southwell and his Ladie

I.

Now, now's the time; so oft by truth
  Promis'd sho'd come to crown your youth.
  Then Faire ones, doe not wrong
  Your joyes, by staying long:
  Or let Love's fire goe out,

Carmen 61.

En tibi domus ut potens
et beata viri tui,
quae tibi sine serviat
(o Hymen Hymenaee io,
o Hymen Hymenaee)

usque dum tremulum movens
cana tempus anilitas
omnia omnibus adnuit.
O Hymen Hymenaee io,
o Hymen Hymenaee.

Transfer omine cum bono
limen aureolos pedes
rasilemque subi forem.
O Hymen Hymenaee io,
o Hymen Hymenaee.

Adspice unus ut accubans
vir tuus Tyrio in toro
totus immineat tibi.
O Hymen Hymenaee io,
o Hymen Hymenaee.

Illi non minus ac tibi
pectore uritur intimo
flamma, sed penite magis.
O Hymen Hymenaee io,
o Hymen Hymenaee.

By lingring thus in doubt:
But learn, that Time once lost,
Is ne'r redeem'd by cost.
Then away; come, *Hymen* guide
To the bed, the bashfull Bride.

II.

Is it (sweet maid) your fault these holy
Bridall-Rites goe on so slowly?
Deare, is it this you dread,
The losse of Maiden-head?
Beleeve me; you will most
Esteeme it when 'tis lost:
Then it no longer keep,
Lest Issue lye asleep.
Then away; come, *Hymen* guide
To the bed, the bashfull Bride.

III.

These Precious-Pearly-Purling teares,
But spring from ceremonious feares.
And 'tis but Native shame,
That hides the loving flame:
And may a while controule
The soft and am'rous soule;
But yet, Loves fire will wast
Such bashfulnesse at last.
Then away; come, *Hymen* guide
To the bed, the bashfull Bride.

IV.

Night now hath watch'd her self half blind;
Yet not a Maiden-head resign'd!
'Tis strange, ye will not flie
To Love's sweet mysterie.
Might yon Full-Moon the sweets
Have, promis'd to your sheets;
She soon wo'd leave her spheare,
To be admitted there.
Then away; come, *Hymen* guide
To the bed, the bashfull Bride.

Carmen 61.

Mitte bracchiolum teres,
praetextate, puellulae.
Iam cubile adeat viri.
O Hymen Hymenaee io,
    o Hymen Hymenaee.

Vos bonae senibus viris
cognitae bene feminae,
collocate puellulam.
O Hymen Hymenaee io,
    o Hymen Hymenaee.

Iam licet venias, marite.
Uxor in thalamo tibi est,
ore floridulo nitens
alba parthenice velut
    luteumve papaver.

At, marite, (ita me iuvent
caelites) nihilo minus
pulcher es, neque te Venus
neglegit. Sed abit dies;
    perge, ne remorare.

V.

On, on devoutly, make no stay;
While *Domiduca* leads the way:
  And *Genius* who attends
  The bed for luckie ends:
  With *Juno* goes the houres,
  And Graces strewing flowers.
  And the boyes with sweet tune sing,
  Hymen, O *Hymen* bring
Home the Turtles; *Hymen* guide
To the bed, the bashfull Bride.

VI.

Behold! how *Hymens* Taper-light
Shews you how much is spent of night.
  See, see the Bride-grooms Torch
  Halfe wasted in the porch.
  And now those Tapers five
  That shew the womb shall thrive:
  Their silv'rie flames advance,
  To tell all prosp'rous chance
Still shall crown the happy life
Of the good man and the wife.

VII.

Move forward then your Rosie feet,
And make, what ere they touch, turn sweet.
  May all, like flowrie Meads
  Smell, where your soft foot treads;
  And every thing assume
  To it, the like perfume:
  As *Zephirus* when he 'spires
  Through *Woodbine*, and *Sweet-bryers*.
Then away; come *Hymen*, guide
To the bed, the bashfull Bride.

Carmen 61.

Non diu remoratus es;
iam venis. Bona te Venus
iuverit, quoniam palam
quod cupis capis et bonum
non abscondis amorem.

Ille pulveris Africi
siderumque micantium
subducat numerum prius,
qui vestri numerare vult
multa milia ludi.

Ludite, ut libet, et brevi
liberos date. Non decet
tam vetus sine liberis
nomen esse, sed indidem
semper ingenerari.

Torquatus volo parvulus
matris e gremio suae
porrigens teneras manus
dulce rideat ad patrem
semihiante labello.

VIII.

And now the yellow Vaile, at last,
Over her fragrant cheek is cast.
Now seems she to expresse
A bashfull willingnesse:
Shewing a heart consenting;
As with a will repenting.
Then gently lead her on
With wise suspicion:
For that, Matrons say, a measure
Of that Passion sweetens Pleasure.

IX.

You, you that be of her neerest kin,
Now o're the threshold force her in.
But to avert the worst;
Let her, her fillets first
Knit to the posts: this point
Remembring, to anoint
The sides: for 'tis a charme
Strong against future harme,
And the evil deads, the which
There was hidden by the Witch.

X.

O *Venus*! thou, to whom is known
The best way how to loose the Zone
Of Virgins! Tell the Maid,
She need not be afraid:
And bid the Youth apply
Close kisses, if she cry:
And charge, he not forbears
Her, though she wooe with teares.
Tel them, now they must adventer,
Since that Love and Night bid enter.

Sit suo similis patri
Manlio et facile insciis
noscitetur ab omnibus
et pudicitiam suae
    matris indicet ore.

Talis illius a bona
matre laus genus approbet,
qualis unica ab optima
matre Telemacho manet
    fama Penelopeo.

Claudite ostia, virgines:
lusimus satis. At, boni
coniuges, bene vivite et
munere assiduo valentem
    exercete iuventam.

XI.

No Fatal Owle the Bedsted keeps,
With direful notes to fright your sleeps:
    No Furies, here about,
    To put the Tapers out,
    Watch, or did make the bed:
    'Tis *Omen* full of dread:
    But all faire signs appeare
    Within the Chamber here.
Juno here, far off, doth stand,
Cooling sleep with charming wand.

XII.

Virgins, weep not; 'twill come, when,
As she, so you'l be ripe for men.
   Then grieve her not, with saying
    She must no more a Maying:
    Or by Rose-buds devine,
    Who'l be her Valentine.
    Nor name those wanton reaks
    Y'ave had at Barly-breaks.
But now kisse her, and thus say,
Take time Lady while ye may.

XIII

Now barre the doors, the Bride-groom puts
The eager Boyes to gather Nuts.
    And now, both Love and Time
    To their full height doe clime:
    O! give them active heat
    And moisture, both compleat:
    Fit Organs for encrease,
    To keep, and to release
That, which may the honour'd Stem
Circle with a Diadem.

XIV.

And now, Behold! the Bed or Couch
That ne'r knew Brides, or Bride-grooms touch,
    Feels in it selfe a fire;
    And tickled with Desire,
    Pants with a Downie brest,
    As with a heart possest:
    Shrugging as it did move,
    Ev'n with the soule of love.
And (oh!) had it but a tongue,
Doves, 'two'd say, yee bill too long.

XV.

O enter then! but see ye shun
A sleep, untill the act be dône.
    Let kisses, in their close,
    Breathe as the Damask Rose:
    Or sweet, as is that gumme
    Doth from *Panchaia* come.
    Teach Nature now to know,
    Lips can make Cherries grow
Sooner, then she, ever yet,
In her wisdome co'd beget.

XVI

On your minutes, hours, dayes, months, years,
Drop the fat blessing of the sphears.
    That good, which Heav'n can give
    To make you bravely live;
    Fall, like a spangling dew,
    By day, and night on you.
    May Fortunes Lilly-hand
    Open at your command;
With all luckie Birds to side
With the Bride-groom, and the Bride.

XVII

Let bounteous Fate your spindles full
Fill, and winde up with whitest wooll.
    Let them not cut the thred
    Of life, untill ye bid.
    May Death yet come at last;
    And not with desp'rate hast:
    But when ye both can say,
    Come, Let us now away.
Be ye to the Barn then born,
Two, like two ripe shocks of corn.

From *A Nuptiall Song, or Epithalamie, on Sir Clipseby Crew and his Lady*

4. *Himen, O Himen!* tread the sacred ground;
Shew thy white feet, and head with Marjoram crown'd:
    Mount up thy flames, and let thy Torch
    Display the Bridegroom in the porch,
        In his desires
More towring, more disparkling then thy fires: . . .

Phineas Fletcher (1582—1650)

From *An Hymen at the Marriage of my most deare Cousins Mr. W. and M. R.*

Hymen, the tier of hearts already tied;
Hymen, the end of lovers never ending;
Hymen, the cause of joyes, joyes never tried,
Joyes never to be spent, yet ever spending:
Hymen, that sow'st with men the desert sands;
Come, bring with thee, come bring thy sacred bands:
Hymen, come *Hymen*, th' hearts are joyn'd, joyn thou the hands.
. . . .
See where he goes, how all the troop he cheereth,
Clad with a saffron coat, in's hand a light;
In all his brow not one sad cloud appeareth:
His coat all pure, his torch all burning bright.
Now chant we *Hymen*, shepherds; *Hymen* sing:
See where he goes, as fresh as is the Spring.
Hymen, oh *Hymen*, *Hymen*, all the valleys ring.

Carmen 62.

IUVENES

Vesper adest, iuvenes, consurgite: Vesper Olympo
exspectata diu vix tandem lumina tollit.
Surgere iam tempus, iam pinguis linquere mensas:
iam veniet virgo, iam dicetur hymenaeus.
Hymen o Hymenaee, Hymen ades o Hymenaee.

VIRGINES

Cernitis, innuptae, iuvenes? Consurgite contra:
nimirum Oetaeos ostendit Noctifer ignes.
Sic certe est. Viden ut perniciter exsiluere?
Non temere exsiluere; canent quod vincere par est.
Hymen o Hymenaee, Hymen ades o Hymenaee.

IUVENES

Non facilis nobis, aequales, palma parata est;
adspicite, innuptae secum ut meditata requirunt.
Non frustra meditantur: habent memorabile quod sit;
nec mirum, penitus quae tota mente laborant.
Nos alio mentes, alio divisimus aures.
Iure igitur vincemur; amat victoria curam.
Quare nunc animos saltem convertite vestros:
dicere iam incipient, iam respondere decebit.
Hymen o Hymenaee, Hymen ades o Hymenaee.

VIRGINES

Hespere, qui caelo fertur crudelior ignis?
Qui natam possis complexu avellere matris,
complexu matris retinentem avellere natam
et iuveni ardenti castam donare puellam.
Quid faciunt hostes capta crudelius urbe?
Hymen o Hymenaee, Hymen ades o Hymenaee.

IUVENES

Hespere, qui caelo lucet iucundior ignis?
Qui desponsa tua firmes conubia flamma,
quae pepigere viri, pepigerunt ante parentes,

EDMUND SPENSER (1552?-1599)

Faerie Queene, II, 12, 74f. (From Tasso, *G. L.* XVI, 14).

The whiles some one did chaunt this lovely lay:
Ah! see, whoso fayre thing doest faine to see,
In springing flowre the image of thy day.
Ah! see the Virgin Rose, how sweetly shee
Doth first peepe foorth with bashfull modestee,
That fairer seemes the lesse ye see her may.
Lo! see soone after how more bold and free
Her bared bosome she doth broad display;
Lo! see soone after how she fades and falls away.

So passeth, in the passing of a day,
Of mortall life the leafe, the bud, the flowre;
Ne more doth florish after first decay,
That earst was sought to deck both bed and bowre
Of many a lady, and many a Paramowre.
Gather therefore the Rose whilest yet is prime,
For soone comes age that will her pride deflowre;
Gather the Rose of love whilest yet is time,
Whilest loving thou mayst loved be with equall crime.

THOMAS CAMPION (1567?-1619)

From *A Description of a Maske in honour of the Lord Hayes and his Bride*, 1607

The song in forme of a Dialogue

Cantor Who is the happier of the two,
A maide, or wife?
Tenor Which is more to be desired,
Peace or strife?
Cantor What strife can be where two are one,
Or what delight to pine alone?
Bass None such true freendes, none so sweet life,
As that between the man and wife.
Tenor A maide is free, a wife is tyed.
Cantor No maide but faine would be a Bride.
Tenor Why live so many single then?
'Tis not I hope for want of men.

Carmen 62.

nec iunxere prius quam se tuus extulit ardor.
Quid datur a divis felici optatius hora?
Hymen o Hymenaee, Hymen ades o Hymenaee.

VIRGINES

Hesperus e nobis, aequales, abstulit unam.
. . . .

IUVENES

. . . .

Namque tuo adventu vigilat custodia semper.
Nocte latent fures, quos idem saepe revertens,
Hespere, mutato comprendis nomine eosdem.
At libet innuptis ficto te carpere questu.
Quid tum, si carpunt tacita quem mente requirunt?
Hymen o Hymenaee, Hymen ades o Hymenaee.

VIRGINES

Ut flos in saeptis secretus nascitur hortis,
ignotus pecori, nullo contusus aratro,
quem mulcent aurae, firmat sol, educat imber;
multi illum pueri, multae optavere puellae;
idem cum tenui carptus defloruit ungui,
nulli illum pueri, nullae optavere puellae,—
sic virgo, dum intacta manet, dum cara suis est.
Cum castum amisit polluto corpore florem,
nec pueris iucunda manet nec cara puellis.
Hymen o Hymenaee, Hymen ades o Hymenaee.

IUVENES

Ut vidua in nudo vitis quae nascitur arvo
numquam se extollit, numquam mitem educat uvam,
sed tenerum prono deflectens pondere corpus
iam iam contingit summum radice flagellum;
hanc nulli agricolae, nulli coluere iuvenci;
at si forte eadem est ulmo coniuncta marito,
multi illam agricolae, multi coluere iuvenci,—

Cantor The bow and arrow both may fit,
And yet 'tis hard the marke to hit.
Bass He levels faire that by his side
Laies at night his lovely Bride.
Cho. Sing Io; Hymen, Io; Io; Hymen.

. . . .

Flora Virginitie is a voluntary powre,
Free from constraint, even like an untoucht flower
Meete to be gather'd when 'tis throughly blowne.

. . . .

A Diologue of foure voices, two Bases and two Trebles

1 Of all the starres which is the kindest
To a loving Bride?
2 *Hesperus* when in the west
He doth the day from night devide.
1 What message can be more respected
Then that which tells wish't ioyes shalbe effected?
2 Do not Brides watch the evening starre?
1 O they can discerne it farre.
2 Love Bridegroomes revels?
1 But for fashion.
2 And why? 1 They hinder wisht occasion.
2 Longing hearts and new delights,
Love short dayes and long nights.

Chorus: *Hesperus*, since you all starres excell
In Bridall kindnes, kindly farewell, farewell.

BEN JONSON (1573?-1637)

From *The Hue and Cry after Cupid*, 1608

Up, youths and virgins, up, and praise
The god whose nights outshine his days;
Hymen, whose hallowed rites
Could never boast of brighter lights;
Whose bands pass liberty.

sic virgo, dum intacta manet, dum inculta senescit.
Cum par conubium maturo tempore adepta est,
cara viro magis et minus est invisa parenti.
Et tu ne pugna cum tali coniuge, virgo.
Non aequum est pugnare, pater cui tradidit ipse,
ipse pater cum matre, quibus parere necesse est.
Virginitas non tota tua est, ex parte parentum est:
tertia pars patri, pars est data tertia matri,
tertia sola tua est. Noli pugnare duobus
qui genero sua iura simul cum dote dederunt.
Hymen o Hymenaee, Hymen ades o Hymenaee.

Two of your troop, that with the morn were free,
  Are now waged to his war.
    And what they are,
  If you'll perfection see,
    Yourselves must be.
Shine, Hesperus, shine forth, thou wished star!

What joy or honours can compare
With holy nuptials, when they are
  Made out of equal parts
Of years, of states, of hands, of hearts!
  When in the happy choice
The spouse and spoused have the foremost voice!
  Such, glad of Hymen's war,
    Live what they are,
  And long perfection see:
    And such ours be.
Shine, Hesperus, shine forth, thou wished star!

The solemn state of this one night
Were fit to last an age's light;
  But there are rites behind
Have less of state, but more of kind:
  Love's wealthy crop of kisses,
And fruitful harvest of his mother's blisses.
  Sound then to Hymen's war:
    That what these are,
  Who will perfection see,
    May haste to be.
Shine, Hesperus, shine forth, thou wished star!

Love's commonwealth consists of toys;
His council are those antic boys,
  Games, Laughter, Sports, Delights,
That triumph with him on these nights;
  To whom we must give way,
For now their reign begins, and lasts till day.
  They sweeten Hymen's war,
    And in that jar,
  Make all that married be

Perfection see.
Shine, Hesperus, shine forth, thou wished star!

Why stays the bridegroom to invade
Her that would be a matron made?
Good-night whilst yet we may
Good-night to you a virgin say:
Tomorrow rise the same
Your mother is, and use a nobler name.
Speed well in Hymen's war,
That, what you are,
By your perfection we
And all may see.
Shine, Hesperus, shine forth, thou wished star!

To-night is Venus' vigil kept
This night no bridegroom ever slept;
And if the fair bride do,
The married say, 'tis his fault too.
Wake then, and let your lights
Wake too; for they'll tell nothing of your nights.
But that in Hymen's war
You perfect are.
And such perfection we
Do pray should be.
Shine, Hesperus, shine forth, thou wished star!

That ere the rosy-fingered morn
Behold nine moons, there may be born
A babe, t'uphold the fame
Of Ratcliffe's blood and Ramsey's name:
That may in his great seed,
Wear the long honours of his father's deed.
Such fruits of Hymen's war
Most perfect are;
And all perfection we
Wish you should see.
Shine, Hesperus, shine forth, thou wished star!

BEN JONSON (1573?-1637)

From *The Barriers*

Opinion

Look, how a flower that close in closes grows,
Hid from rude cattle, bruised with no ploughs,
Which th'air doth stroke, sun strengthen, showers shoot higher,
It many youths and many maids desire;
The same when cropt by cruel hand is withered,
No youths at all, no maidens have desired:
So a virgin, while untouched she doth remain,
Is dear to hers; but when with body's stain
Her chaster flower is lost, she leaves to appear
Or sweet to young men, or to maidens dear.
That conquest then may crown me in this war,
Virgins, O virgins, fly from Hymen far.

Truth

Virgins, O virgins, to sweet Hymen yield.
For as a lone vine in a naked field
Never extols her branches, never bears
Ripe grapes, but with a headlong heaviness wears
Her tender body, and her highest sprout
Is quickly levelled with her fading root;
By whom no husbandman, no youths will dwell;
But if by fortune she be married well
To the elm her husband, many husbandmen
And many youths inhabit by her then:
So whilst a virgin doth untouched abide,
All unmanured, she grows old with her pride;
But when to equal wedlock, in fit time,
Her fortune and endeavour lets her climb,
Dear to her love and parents she is held.
Virgins, O virgins, to sweet Hymen yield.

WILLIAM SHAKESPEARE (1564-1616)

Tempest IV, 1, 1ff.

Prospero If I have too austerely punish'd you,
Your compensation makes amends; for I
Have given you here a third of mine own life,
Or that for which I live . . .

GEORGE CHAPMAN (1559?-1634), in his continuation of Marlowe's *Hero and Leander*.

From *Epithalamium Teratos*, 1598

The evening star I see:
Rise, youths, the evening star
Helps Love to summon war;
Both now embracing be.

Rise, youths, Love's rite claims more than banquets, rise!
Now the bright marigolds that deck the skies,
Phoebus' celestial flowers that, contrary
To his flowers here, ope when he shuts his eye,
And shut when he doth open, crown your sports:
Now Love in night, and night in Love exhorts
Courtship and dances: all your parts employ,
And suit night's rich expansure with your joy.
Love paints his longings in sweet virgins' eyes:
Rise, youths, Love's rite claims more than banquets, rise!

Rise, virgins! let fair nuptial loves enfold
Your fruitless breasts: the maidenheads ye hold
Are not your own alone, but parted are;
Part in disposing them your parents share,
And that a third part is; so must ye save
Youı loves a third, and you your thirds must have.
Love paints his longings in sweet virgins' eyes:
Rise, youths, Love's rite claims more than banquets, rise!

From *A Hymn to Hymen for the Nuptials of Princess Elizabeth, daughter of James 1, with Count Palatine of the Rhine, 1613*

And as the tender hyacinth, that grows
Where Phoebus most his golden beams bestows,
Is propt with care, is watered every hour,—
The sweet winds adding their increasing power,
The scattered drops of night's refreshing dew
Hasting the full grace of his glorious hue,—
Which, once disclosing, must be gathered straight,
Or hue and colour both will lose their height:
So, of a virgin, high, and richly kept,
The grace and sweetness full grown must be reaped,
Or forth her spirits fly in empty air;
The sooner fading, the more sweet and fair.
Gentle, O gentle Hymen, be not then
Cruel that kindest art to maids and men.

Alphonsus V, 1 ff.

Let guilty minds tremble at sight of death.
My heart is of the nature of the palm
Not to be broken till the highest bud
Be bent and tied unto the lowest root.

THOMAS OTWAY (1652-1685)

From *The Orphan*, IV, 2

You took her up a little tender flower,
Just sprouted on a bank, which the next frost
Had nipp'd; and, with a careful loving hand,
Transplanted her into your own fair garden,
Where the sun always shines: there long she flourish'd,
Grew sweet to sense, and lovely to the eye,
'Till at the last a cruel spoiler came,
Cropp'd this fair rose, and rifled all its sweetness,
Then cast it like a loathsome weed away.

JOHN GAY (1685-1732)

Beggar's Opera, Act 1, Air VI

Virgins are like the fair flower in its lustre,
  Which in the garden enamels the ground;
Near it the bees in play flutter and cluster,
  And gaudy butterflies frolic around.
But when once pluck'd 'tis no longer alluring,
  To Covent Garden 'tis sent (as yet sweet),
There fades, and shrinks, and grows past all enduring,
  Rots, stinks, and dies, and is trod under feet.

ALFRED TENNYSON (1809-1892)

From *In Memoriam*, CXXI

Sweet Hesper-Phosphor, double name
  For what is one, the first, the last,
  Thou, like my present and my past,
Thy place is changed; thou art the same.

Carmen 63 (lines 1-23)

Super alta vectus Attis celeri rate maria,
Phrygium ut nemus citato cupide pede tetigit
adiitque opaca silvis redimita loca deae,
stimulatus ibi furenti rabie, vagus animis,
devolvit ili acuto sibi pondera silice.
Itaque ut relicta sensit sibi membra sine viro,
etiam recente terrae sola sanguine maculans,
niveis citata cepit manibus leve tympanum,
tympanum, tubam Cybelles, tua, mater, initia,
quatiensque terga tauri teneris cava digitis,
canere haec suis adorta est tremebunda comitibus:
"Agite, ite ad alta, Gallae, Cybeles nemora simul,
simul ite, Dindymenae dominae vaga pecora,
aliena quae petentes velut exsules loca,
sectam meam exsecutae duce me, mihi comites,
rapidum salum tulistis truculentaque pelagi
et corpus evirastis Veneris nimio odio;
hilarate erae citatis erroribus animum.
Mora tarda mente cedat; simul ite, sequimini
Phrygiam ad domum Cybelles, Phrygia ad nemora deae,
ubi cymbalum sonat vox, ubi tympana reboant,
tibicen ubi canit Phryx curvo grave calamo,
ubi capita Maenades vi iaciunt hederigerae,
. . . .

ALGERNON CHARLES SWINBURNE (1837-1909)

From *Dolores*

Cry aloud; for the old world is broken:
    Cry out; for the Phrygian is priest,
And rears not the bountiful token
    And spreads not the fatherly feast.
From the midmost of Ida, from shady
    Recesses that murmur at morn,
They have brought and baptized her, Our Lady,
    A goddess new-born.

And the chaplets of old are above us,
    And the oyster-bed teems out of reach;
Old poets outsing and outlove us,
    And Catullus makes mouths at our speech.
Who shall kiss, in thy father's own city,
    With such lips as he sang with, again?
Intercede for us all of thy pity,
        Our Lady of Pain.

Out of Dindymus heavily laden
    Her lions draw bound and unfed
A mother, a mortal, a maiden,
    A queen over death and the dead.
She is cold, and her habit is lowly,
    Her temple of branches and sods;
Most fruitful and virginal, holy,
    A mother of gods.

GEORGE MEREDITH (1828-1909)

From *Phaëthôn*

(Attempted in the galliambic measure)

At the coming up of Phoebus the all-luminous charioteer,
Double-visaged stand the mountains in imperial multitudes,
And with shadows dappled men sing to him, Hail, O Beneficent!
For they shudder chill, the earth-vales, at his clouding, shudder [to black;
In the light of him there is music thro' the poplar and river- [sedge,
Renovation, chirp of brooks, hum of the forest—an ocean-song.

ALFRED TENNYSON (1809-1892)

From *Boädicea* in Galliambic metre

While I roved about the forest, long and bitterly meditating,
There I heard them in the darkness, at the mystical ceremony,
Loosely robed in flying raiment, sang the terrible prophetesses,
"Fear not, isle of blowing woodland, isle of silvery parapets!
Tho' the Roman eagle shadow thee, tho' the gathering enemy [narrow thee,
Thou shalt wax and he shall dwindle, thou shalt be the mighty one yet!
Thine the liberty, thine the glory, thine the deeds to be cele- [brated,
Thine the myriad-rolling ocean, light and shadow illimitable,
Thine the lands of lasting summer, many-blossoming Paradises,
Thine the North and thine the South and thine the battle- [thunder of God."
So they chanted: how shall Britain light upon auguries happier?
So they chanted in the darkness, and there cometh a victory [now.

Carmen 64 (lines 1164 : 304-306)

Peliaco quondam prognatae vertice pinus
dicuntur liquidas Neptuni nasse per undas
Phasidos ad fluctus et fines Aeetaeos,
cum lecti iuvenes, Argivae robora pubis,
auratam optantes Colchis avertere pellem
ausi sunt vada salsa cita decurrere puppi,
caerula verrentes abiegnis aequora palmis.
Diva quibus retinens in summis urbibus arces,
ipsa levi fecit volitantem flamine currum,
pinea coniungens inflexae texta carinae.
Illa rudem cursu prima imbuit Amphitriten.
Quae simul ac rostro ventosum proscidit aequor
tortaque remigio spumis incanuit unda,
emersere feri candenti e gurgite vultus
aequoreae monstrum Nereides admirantes.
Illa, si qua alia, viderunt luce marinas
mortales oculi nudato corpore Nymphas
nutricum tenus exstantes e gurgite cano.
Tum Thetidis Peleus incensus fertur amore,
tum Thetis humanos non despexit hymenaeos,
tum Thetidi pater ipse iugandum Pelea sensit.
O nimis optato saeclorum tempore nati
heroes, salvete, deum genus! O bona matrum
progenies, salvete iterum! . . .
Vos ego saepe meo vos carmine compellabo;
teque adeo eximie taedis felicibus aucte,
Thessaliae columen, Peleu, cui Iuppiter ipse,
ipse suos divum genitor concessit amores.
Tene Thetis tenuit pulcherrima Nereine?
Tene suam Tethys concessit ducere neptem
Oceanusque, mari totum qui amplectitur orbem?
Quae simul optatae finito tempore luces
advenere, domum conventu tota frequentat
Thessalia, oppletur laetanti regia coetu;
dona ferunt prae se, declarant gaudia vultu.
Deseritur Cieros, linquunt Phthiotica Tempe
Crannonisque domos ac moenia Larisaea,
Pharsaliam coeunt, Pharsalia tecta frequentant.

EDMUND SPENSER (1552?-1599)

Faerie Queene, VII, 7, 12

Was never so great joyance since the day
That all the gods whylome assembled were
On Haemus hill in their divine array,
To celebrate the solemn bridall cheare
Twixt Peleus and Dame Thetis pointed there;
Where Phoebus selfe, that god of Poets hight,
They say, did sing the spousall hymne full cleere,
That all the gods were ravisht with delight
Of his celestiall song, and Musicks wondrous might.

WILLIAM SHAKESPEARE (1564-1616)

Tempest III, 1, 83ff.

Miranda I am your wife, if you will marry me;
If not, I'll die your maid: to be your fellow
You may deny me; but I'll be your servant,
Whether you will or no.

FRANCIS BEAUMONT (1584-1616) AND JOHN FLETCHER (1579-1625) *Maid's Tragedy*, II, 2

Aspatia But where's the lady?
Antiphila There, madam!
Aspatia Fie! you have missed it here, Antiphila,
You are much mistaken, wench;
These colours are not dull and pale enough
To show a soul so full of misery
As this sad lady's was. Do it by me,
Do it again by me, the lost Aspatia;
And you shall find all true but the wild island.
Suppose I stand upon the sea-beach now,
Mine arms thus, and my hair blown with the wind,
Wild as that desert; and let all about me
Tell that I am forsaken. Do my face,
(If thou hadst ever feeling of a sorrow)
Thus, thus, Antiphila; strive to make me look
Like Sorrow's monument; and the trees about me,

Rura colit nemo, mollescunt colla iuvencis,
non humilis curvis purgatur vinea rastris,
non glaebam prono convellit vomere taurus,
non falx attenuat frondatorum arboris umbram,
squalida desertis rubigo infertur aratris.
Ipsius at sedes, quacumque opulenta recessit
regia, fulgenti splendent auro atque argento.
Candet ebur soliis, collucent pocula mensae,
tota domus gaudet regali splendida gaza.
Pulvinar vero divae geniale locatur
sedibus in mediis, Indo quod dente politum
tincta tegit roseo conchyli purpura fuco.
Haec vestis priscis hominum variata figuris
heroum mira virtutes indicat arte:
namque fluentisono prospectans litore Diae,
Thesea cedentem celeri cum classe tuetur
indomitos in corde gerens Ariadna furores,
necdum etiam sese quae visit visere credit,
ut pote fallaci quae tum primum excita somno
desertam in sola miseram se cernat harena.
Immemor at iuvenis fugiens pellit vada remis,
inrita ventosae linquens promissa procellae.
Quem procul ex alga maestis Minois ocellis,
saxea ut effigies bacchantis, prospicit, eheu,
prospicit et magnis curarum fluctuat undis,
non flavo retinens subtilem vertice mitram,
non contecta levi velatum pectus amictu,
non tereti strophio lactentis vincta papillas,
omnia quae toto delapsa e corpore passim
ipsius ante pedes fluctus salis adludebant.
Sed neque tum mitrae neque tum fluitantis amictus
illa vicem curans toto ex te pectore, Theseu,
toto animo, tota pendebat perdita mente.
A! misera, assiduis quam luctibus exsternavit
spinosas Erycina serens in pectore curas,
illa tempestate, ferox quo ex tempore Theseus
egressus curvis e litoribus Piraei
attigit iniusti regis Gortynia tecta.
Nam perhibent olim crudeli peste coactam
Androgeoneae poenas exsolvere caedis

Let them be dry and leafless; let the rocks
Groan with continual surges; and behind me
Make all a desolation. See, see, wenches,
A miserable life of this poor picture!

THOMAS CAMPION (1567?-1619)

Description of a Maske at the Marriage of the Earle of Somerset,
Printed 1614.

Song

Goe, happy man, like th' Evening Starre,
Whose beames to Bride-groomes well-come are: . . .

The Second Squire

All blessings which the *Fates*, Propheticke, sung,
At *Peleus* Nuptialls, and what ever tongue
Can figure more, this night, and aye betide,
The honour'd Bride-groome and the honour'd Bride.

ALFRED TENNYSON (1809-1892)

From *Lancelot and Elaine*

but when now the lords and dames
And people, from the high door streaming, brake
Disorderly, as homeward each . . .

From the same

And Lancelot answer'd, "Had I chosen to wed,
I had been wedded earlier, sweet Elaine;
But now there never will be wife of mine."
"No, no," she cried, "I care not to be wife,
But to be with you still, to see your face,
To serve you, and to follow you thro' the world."

electos iuvenes simul et decus innuptarum
Cecropiam solitam esse dapem dare Minotauro.
Quis angusta malis cum moenia vexarentur,
ipse suum Theseus pro caris corpus Athenis
proicere optavit potius quam talia Cretam
funera Cecropiae nec funera portarentur.
Atque ita nave levi nitens ac lenibus auris
magnanimum ad Minoa venit sedesque superbas.
Hunc simul ac cupido conspexit lumine virgo
regia, quam suavis exspirans castus odores
lectulus in molli complexu matris alebat,
quales Eurotae progignunt flumina myrtos
aurave distinctos educit verna colores,
non prius ex illo flagrantia declinavit
lumina, quam cuncto concepit corpore flammam
funditus atque imis exarsit tota medullis.
Heu misere exagitans immiti corde furores,
sancte puer, curis hominum qui gaudia misces,
quaeque regis Golgos quaeque Idalium frondosum,
qualibus incensam iactastis mente puellam
fluctibus, in flavo saepe hospite suspirantem!
Quantos illa tulit languenti corde timores!
Quanto saepe magis fulgore expalluit auri,
cum saevum cupiens contra contendere monstrum
aut mortem appeteret Theseus aut praemia laudis!
Non ingrata tamen frustra munuscula divis
promittens tacito succendit vota labello.
Nam velut in summo quatientem bracchia Tauro
quercum aut conigeram sudanti cortice pinum,
indomitus turbo contorquens flamine robur
eruit (illa procul radicitus exturbata
prona cadit, late quaeviscumque obvia frangens),
sic domito saevum prostravit corpore Theseus
nequiquam vanis iactantem cornua ventis.
Inde pedem sospes multa cum laude reflexit
errabunda regens tenui vestigia filo,
ne labyrintheis e flexibus egredientem
tecti frustraretur inobservabilis error.

JAMES ELROY FLECKER (1884-1915)

Epithalamion

Smile then, children, hand in hand
Bright and white as the summer snow,
Or that young King of the Grecian land,
Who smiled on Thetis, long ago,—
So long ago when, heart aflame,
The grave and gentle Peleus came
To the shore where the halcyon flies
To wed the maiden of his devotion,
The dancing lady with sky-blue eyes,
Thetis, the darling of Paradise,
The daughter of old Ocean.
Seas before her rise and break,
Dolphins tumble in her wake
Along the sapphire courses:
With Tritons ablow on their pearly shells
With a plash of waves and a clash of bells
From the glimmering house where her Father dwells
She drives his white-tail horses!
And the boys of heaven gowned and crowned,
Have Aphrodite to lead them round,
Aphrodite with hair unbound
Her silver breasts adorning.
Her long, her soft, her streaming hair,
Falls on a silver breast laid bare
By the stir and swing of the sealit air
And the movement of the morning.

Sed quid ego a primo digressus carmine plura
commemorem, ut linquens genitoris filia vultum,
ut consanguineae complexum, ut denique matris,
quae misera in nata deperdita lamentata est,
omnibus his Thesei dulcem praeoptarit amorem;
aut ut vecta ratis spumosa ad litora Diae
venerit, aut ut eam devinctam lumina somno
liquerit immemori discedens pectore coniunx?
Saepe illam perhibent ardenti corde furentem
clarisonas imo fudisse e pectore voces,
ac tum praeruptos tristem conscendere montes
unde aciem in pelagi vastos protenderet aestus,
tum tremuli salis adversas procurrere in undas
mollia nudatae tollentem tegmina surae
atque haec extremis maestam dixisse querelis,
frigidulos udo singultus ore cientem:
"Sicine me patriis avectam, perfide, ab aris,
perfide, deserto liquisti in litore, Theseu?
Sicine discedens neglecto numine divum,
immemor a! devota domum periuria portas?
Nullane res potuit crudelis flectere mentis
consilium? Tibi nulla fuit clementia praesto,
immite ut nostri vellet miserescere pectus?
At non haec quondam blanda promissa dedisti
voce mihi; non haec misere sperare iubebas,
sed conubia laeta, sed optatos hymenaeos,
quae cuncta aerii discerpunt inrita venti.
Tum iam nulla viro iuranti femina credat,
nulla viri speret sermones esse fideles;
quis dum aliquid cupiens animus praegestit apisci,
nil metuunt iurare, nihil promittere parcunt;
sed simul ac cupidae mentis satiata libido est,
dicta nihil metuere, nihil periuria curant.
Certe ego te in medio versantem turbine leti
eripui et potius germanum amittere crevi,
quam tibi fallaci supremo in tempore deessem.
Pro quo dilaceranda feris dabor alitibusque
praeda neque iniecta tumulabor mortua terra.
Quaenam te genuit sola sub rupe leaena,

quod mare conceptum spumantibus exspuit undis,
quae Syrtis, quae Scylla rapax, quae vasta Charybdis,
talia qui reddis pro dulci praemia vita?
Si tibi non cordi fuerant conubia nostra,
saeva quod horrebas prisci praecepta parentis,
at tamen in vestras potuisti ducere sedes,
quae tibi iucundo famularer serva labore,
candida permulcens liquidis vestigia lymphis
purpureave tuum consternens veste cubile.
Sed quid ego ignaris nequiquam conquerar auris,

. . . .

large multiplici constructae sunt dape mensae,
cum interea infirmo quatientes corpora motu
veridicos Parcae coeperunt edere cantus.

Carmen 65 (lines 1-12)

Etsi me assiduo confectum cura dolore
    sevocat a doctis, Ortale, virginibus,
nec potis est dulcis Musarum expromere fetus
    mens animi (tantis fluctuat ipsa malis:
namque mei nuper Lethaeo in gurgite fratris
    pallidulum manans adluit unda pedem,
Troia Rhoeteo quem subter litore tellus
    ereptum nostris obterit ex oculis.
Adloquar, audiero numquam tua facta loquentem,
    numquam ego te, vita frater amabilior,
adspiciam posthac. At certe semper amabo,
    semper maesta tua carmina morte canam,

. . . .

ROBERT HERRICK (1591-1674)

On himselfe

Aske me, why I do not sing
To the tension of the string,
As I did, not long ago,
When my numbers full did flow?
Griefe (ay me!) hath struck my Lute,
And my tongue at one time mute.

ALFRED TENNYSON (1809-1892)

Praefatory Poem to my Brother's Sonnets

Midnight, June 30, 1879

I

Midnight—in no midsummer tune
The breakers lash the shores:
The cuckoo of a joyless June
Is calling out of doors:

And thou hast vanish'd from thine own
To that which looks like rest,
True brother, only to be known
By those who love thee best.

II

Midnight—and joyless June gone by,
And from the deluged park
The cuckoo of a worse July
Is calling thro' the dark:

But thou art silent underground,
And o'er thee streams the rain,
True poet, surely to be found
When Truth is found again.

III

And, now to these unsummer'd skies
The summer bird is still,
Far off a phantom cuckoo cries
From out a phantom hill;

And thro' this midnight breaks the sun
Of sixty years away,
The light of days when life begun,
The days that seem to-day,

When all my griefs were shared with thee,
As all my hopes were thine—
As all thou wert was one with me,
May all thou art be mine!

Carmen 66 (lines 1-14)

Omnia qui magni dispexit lumina mundi,
qui stellarum ortus comperit atque obitus,
flammeus ut rapidi solis nitor obscuretur,
ut cedant certis sidera temporibus,
ut Triviam furtim sub Latmia saxa relegans
dulcis amor gyro devocet aerio,
idem me ille Conon caelesti in lumine vidit
e Bereniceo vertice caesariem
fulgentem clare, quam multis illa dearum
levia protendens bracchia pollicita est,
qua rex tempestate novo auctus hymenaeo
vastatum finis iverat Assyrios,
dulcia nocturnae portans vestigia rixae
quam de virgineis gesserat exuviis.
. . . .

RICHARD CRASHAW (1613?-1649)

The Teare

II

O, 'tis not a teare:
'Tis a star about to dropp
From thine eye, its spheare;
The sun will stoope and take it up:
Proud will his sister be, to weare
This thine eyes' iewell in her eare.
. . . .

VII

Thus carried up on high
(For to Heaven thou must goe),
Sweetly shalt thou lye,
And in soft slumbers bathe thy woe,
Till the singing orbes awake thee,
And one of their bright chorus make thee.

VIII

There thy selfe shalt bee
An eye, but not a weeping one;
Yet I doubt of thee,
Whether th' had'st rather there have shone
An eye of heaven; or still shine here,
In the heaven of Marie's eye, a TEARE.

ALEXANDER POPE (1688-1744)

From *The Rape of the Lock*

What time would spare, from steel receives its date.
And monuments, like men, submit to fate!
Steel could the labour of the gods destroy,
And strike to dust th' imperial tow'rs of Troy;
Steel could the works of mortal pride confound,
And hew triumphal arches to the ground.
What wonder then, fair nymph! thy hairs should feel
The conqu'ring force of unresisted steel?

Carmen 68 (lines 1-26)

Quod mihi fortuna casuque oppressus acerbo
  conscriptum hoc lacrimis mittis epistolium,
naufragum ut eiectum spumantibus aequoris undis
  sublevem et a mortis limine restituam,
quem neque sancta Venus molli requiescere somno
  desertum in lecto caelibe perpetitur
nec veterum dulci scriptorum carmine Musae
  oblectant, cum mens anxia pervigilat,
id gratum est mihi, me quoniam tibi dicis amicum
  muneraque et Musarum hinc petis et Veneris.
Sed tibi ne mea sint ignota incommoda, Manli,
  neu me odisse putes hospitis officium,
accipe quis merser fortunae fluctibus ipse,
  ne amplius a misero dona beata petas.
Tempore quo primum vestis mihi tradita pura est,
  iucundum cum aetas florida ver ageret,
multa satis lusi; non est dea nescia nostri
  quae dulcem curis miscet amaritiem.
Sed totum hoc studium luctu fraterna mihi mors
  abstulit. O misero frater adempte mihi,
tu mea tu moriens fregisti commoda, frater,
  tecum una tota est nostra sepulta domus;
omnia tecum una perierunt gaudia nostra
  quae tuus in vita dulcis alebat amor.
Cuius ego interitu tota de mente fugavi
  haec studia atque omnis delicias animi.

. . . .

ROBERT HERRICK (1591-1674)

An Ode to Master Endymion Porter, upon his Brothers death

Not all thy flushing Sunnes are set,
Herrick, as yet:
Nor doth this far-drawn Hemisphere
Frown, and look sullen ev'ry where.
Daies may conclude in nights; and Suns may rest,
As dead, within the West;
Yet the next Morne, re-guild the fragrant East.

Alas for me! that I have lost
E'en all almost:
Sunk is my sight; set is my Sun;
And all the loome of life undone:
The staffe, the Elme, the prop, the shelt'ring wall
Whereon my Vine did crawle,
Now, now, blowne downe; needs must the old stock fall.

Yet, *Porter*, while thou keep'st alive,
In death I thrive:
And like a *Phenix* re-aspire
From out my Narde, and Fun'rall fire:
And as I prune my feather'd youth, so I
Doe mar'l how I co'd die,
When I had Thee, my chiefe Preserver, by.

I'm up, I'm up, and blesse that hand,
Which makes me stand
Now as I doe; and but for thee,
I must confesse, I co'd not be.
The debt is paid: for he who doth resigne
Thanks to the gen'rous Vine;
Invites fresh Grapes to fill his Presse with Wine.

Carmen 70.

Nulli se dicit mulier mea nubere malle
 quam mihi, non si se Iuppiter ipse petat.
Dicit; sed mulier cupido quod dicit amanti
 in vento et rapida scribere oportet aqua.

SIR PHILIP SIDNEY (1554-1586)

"Unto nobody" my woman saith, "she had rather a wife be
Than to myself; not though *Jove* grew a suitor of hers."
These be her words, but a woman's words to a love that is eager,
In wind or water's stream do require to be writ.

WILLIAM SHAKESPEARE (1564-1616)

King Henry VIII, IV, 2, 45f.

Griffith Noble madam,
Men's evil manners live in brass; their virtues
We write in water.

Troilus and Cressida, V, 3, 108ff.

Troilus Words, words, mere words, no matter from the heart;
The effect doth operate another way.
(*Tearing the letter.*)
Go, wind, to wind, there turn and change together.
My love with words and errors still she feeds;
But edifies another with her deeds.

WILLIAM BYRD, *Love's Immortality* (from *Psalms, Songs and Sonnets*, 1611)

Crowned with flowers I saw fair Amaryllis
By Thyrsis sit, hard by a fount of crystal;
And with her hand, more white than snow or lilies,
On sand she wrote, "My faith shall be immortal":
And suddenly a storm of wind and weather
Blew all her faith and sand away together.

JOHN DONNE (1573-1631)

From *Elegie* XVI, *The Expostulation*

Are vowes so cheape with women, or the matter
Whereof they are made, that they are writ in water,
And blowne away with winde?

SIR HENRY WOTTON (1568-1639)

From *A Woman's Heart*

Why was she born to please? or I to trust
 Words writ in dust,
Suffering her eyes to govern my despair,
 My pain for air; . . .

BEN JONSON (1573-1637) *Underwoods*

From *An Elegy*

To make the doubt clear, that no woman's true,
Was it my fate to prove it full in you?
Thought I, but one had breathed the purer air,
And must she needs be false, because she's fair?
Is it your beauty's mark, or of your youth,
Or your perfection, not to study truth?
Or think you heaven is deaf, or hath no eyes,
Or those it hath wink at your perjuries?
Are vows so cheap with women? or the matter
Whereof they're made, that they are writ in water,
And blown away with wind? or doth their breath
Both hot and cold at once, threat life and death?

SIR EDWARD SHERBURNE (1618-1702)

Lately by clear Thames's side
Fair Lycoris I espied,
With the pen of her white hand
These words printing on the sand:
"None Lycoris doth approve
But Mirtillo for her love."
Ah, fair nymph!! those words were fit
In sand only to be writ:
For the quickly rising streams
In a little moment's stay
From the shore wash'd clean away
What thy hand had there impress'd,
And Mirtillo from thy breast.

Sir Walter Scott (1771-1832)

From *TheBetrothed*, Ch. XX

Woman's faith, and woman's trust—
Write the characters in dust;
Stamp them on the running stream,
Print them on the moon's pale beam,
And each evanescent letter
Shall be clearer, firmer, better,
And more permanent, I ween,
Than the thing those letters mean.

I have strain'd the spider's thread
'Gainst the promise of a maid;
I have weigh'd a grain of sand
'Gainst her plight of heart and hand;
I told my true love of the token,
How her faith proved light and her word was broken:
Again her word and truth she plight,
And I believed them again ere night.

Carmen 72.

Dicebas quondam solum te nosse Catullum,
  Lesbia, nec prae me velle tenere Iovem.
Dilexi tum te non tantum ut vulgus amicam,
  sed pater ut natos diligit et generos.
Nunc te cognovi; quare etsi impensius uror,
  multo mi tamen es vilior et levior.
"Qui potis est?" inquis. Quod amantem iniuria talis
  cogit amare magis sed bene velle minus.

WILLIAM SHAKESPEARE (1564-1616)

Sonnet CL

O, from what power hast thou this powerful might
With insufficiency my heart to sway?
To make me give the lie to my true sight,
And swear that brightness doth not grace the day?
Whence hast thou this becoming of things ill,
That in the very refuse of thy deeds
There is such strength and warrantise of skill
That, in my mind, thy worst all best exceeds?
Who taught thee how to make me love thee more,
The more I hear and see just cause of hate?
O, though I love what others do abhor,
With others thou shouldst not abhor my state:
If thy unworthiness raised love in me,
More worthy I to be beloved of thee.

RICHARD LOVELACE (1618-1658)

That me alone you lov'd, you once did say,
Nor should I to the king of gods give way.
Then I lov'd thee not as a common dear,
But as a father doth his children chear.
Now thee I know, more bitterly I smart;
Yet thou to me more light and cheaper art.
What pow'r is this? that such a wrong should press
Me to love more, yet wish thee well much lesse.
I hate and love; would'st thou the reason know?
I know not; but I burn, and feel it so.

WILLIAM WALSH (1663-1708)

To his False Mistress

Thou saidst that I alone thy heart could move,
And that for me thou wouldst abandon Jove.
I lov'd thee then, nor with a love defil'd,
But as a father loves his only child.
I know thee now, and though I fiercelier burn,
Thou art become the object of my scorn.
See what thy falsehood gets; I must confess
I love thee more, but I esteem thee less.

Carmen 73.

Desine de quoquam quidquam bene velle mereri
    aut aliquem fieri posse putare pium.
Omnia sunt ingrata, nihil fecisse benigne est;
    immo etiam taedet, taedet obestque magis,
ut mihi, quem nemo gravius nec acerbius urget
    quam modo qui me unum atque unicum amicum
        habuit.

ROBERT HERRICK (1591-1674)

A *Hymne to Sir Clipseby Crew*

'Twas not Lov's Dart;
Or any blow
Of want, or foe,
Did wound my heart
With an eternall smart:

But only you,
My sometimes known
Companion,
(My dearest *Crew*,)
That me unkindly slew.

May your fault dye,
And have no name
In Bookes of fame;
Or let it lye
Forgotten now, as I.

We parted are,
And now no more,
As heretofore,
By jocond Larr,
Shall be familiar.

But though we Sever
My *Crew* shall see,
That I will be
Here faithlesse never;
But love my *Clipseby* ever.

Carmen 74.

Gellius audierat patruum obiurgare solere,
    si quis delicias diceret aut faceret.
Hoc ne ipsi accideret, patrui perdepsuit ipsam
    uxorem et patruum reddidit Harpocratem.
Quod voluit fecit: nam, quamvis inrumet ipsum
    nunc patruum, verbum non faciet patruus.

BEN JONSON (1573?-1637)

Bartholomew Fair, V, 3

(Overdo discloses Littlewit's disguised wife to him)

Lit. O my wife, my wife, my wife!
Over. Is she your wife? *redde te Harpocratem.*

Sejanus, V, 7

Cotta Let me conjure you not to utter it;
For it is trusted to me with that bond.
Latiaris I am Harpocrates.

Carmen 76.

Si qua recordanti benefacta priora voluptas
    est homini, cum se cogitat esse pium,
nec sanctam violasse fidem nec foedere in ullo
    divum ad fallendos numine abusum homines,
multa parata manent in longa aetate, Catulle,
    ex hoc ingrato gaudia amore tibi.
Nam quaecumque homines bene cuiquam aut dicere possunt
    aut facere, haec a te dictaque factaque sunt;
omnia quae ingratae perierunt credita menti.
    Quare cur tu te iam amplius excrucies?
Quin tu animo offirmas atque istinc teque reducis
    et dis invitis desinis esse miser?
Difficile est longum subito deponere amorem;
    difficile est, verum hoc qua libet efficias.
Una salus haec est, hoc est tibi pervincendum;
    hoc facias, sive id non pote sive pote.
O di, si vestrum est misereri aut si quibus umquam
    extremam iam ipsa in morte tulistis opem,
me miserum adspicite et, si vitam puriter egi,
    eripite hanc pestem perniciemque mihi!
Heu mihi subrepens imos ut torpor in artus
    expulit ex omni pectore laetitias.
Non iam illud quaero, contra ut me diligat illa,
    aut, quod non potis est, esse pudica velit:
ipse valere opto et taetrum hunc deponere morbum.
    O di, reddite mi hoc pro pietate mea!

From *Pilkington's Madrigals*, 1613

Why do I fret and grieve
Since she denies and will no comfort give?
O fatal foul decree:
She stops her ears and smiles at my complaint;
Whilst wounded with disdain
I seek all means I can to set me free:
And yet it will not be—
O bitter pain!

THOMAS CAREW (c. 1598-1639)

From *Prayer to the Wind*

Thou can'st kindle hidden flame,
And againe destroy the same:
Then, for pittie, either stir
Up the fire of love in her,
That alike both flames may shine,
Or else quite extinguish mine.

WILLIAM WALSH (1663-1708)

Is there a pious pleasure that proceeds
From contemplation of our virtuous deeds?
That all mean sordid action we despise,
And scorn to gain a throne by cheats and lies?
Thyrsis, thou hast sure blessings laid in store
From thy just dealing in this curst amour.
What honour can in words or deeds be shown
Which to the fair thou hast not said and done?
On her false heart they all are thrown away:
She only swears more easily to betray.
Ye powers that know the many vows she broke,
Free my just soul from this unequal yoke.
My love boils up, and like a raging flood
Runs through my veins and taints my vital blood.
I do not vainly beg she may grow chaste,
Or with an equal passion burn at last—
The one she cannot practise, though she would,
And I contemn the other, though she should—:
Nor ask I vengeance on the perjured jilt;
'Tis punishment enough to have her guilt.
I beg but balsam for my bleeding breast,
Cure for my wounds and from my labours rest.

FANNY GREVILLE (18th Century)

From *Prayer for Indifference*

Sweet airy Being, wanton Spright!
Who liv'st in woods unseen;
And oft, by Cynthia's silver light,
Tripp'st gaily o'er the green:

If e'er thy pitying heart was moved,
As ancient stories tell,
And for th' Athenian Maid who loved,
Thou sought'st a wondrous spell;

O, deign once more t'exert thy power!
Haply, some herb, or tree,
Sovereign as juice from western flower,
Conceals a balm for me.

I ask no kind return in Love;
No tempting charm to please;
Far from the heart such gifts remove,
That sighs for peace and ease.

. . . .

O, haste to shed the sovereign balm,
My shattered nerves new-string;
And for my guest, serenely calm,
The nymph Indifference bring.

Carmen 82.

Quinti, si tibi vis oculos debere Catullum
    aut aliud si quid carius est oculis,
eripere ei noli multo quod carius illi
    est oculis seu quid carius est oculis.

Robert Herrick (1591-1674)

From *To Anthea, who may command him any thing*

Thou are my life, my love, my heart,
The very eyes of me:
And hast command of every part,
To live and die for thee.

Richard Lovelace (1618-1658)

Quintius, if you'l endear Catullus eyes,
Or what he dearer then his eyes doth prize,
Ravish not what is dearer then his eyes,
Or what he dearer then his eyes doth prize.

Carmen 84.

Chommoda dicebat, si quando commoda vellet
    dicere, et insidias Arrius hinsidias,
et tum mirifice sperabat se esse locutum
    cum quantum poterat dixerat hinsidias.
Credo, sic mater, sic liber avunculus eius,
    sic maternus avus dixerat atque avia.
Hoc misso in Syriam requierant omnibus aures:
    audibant eadem haec leniter et leviter,
nec sibi postilla metuebant talia verba,
    cum subito adfertur nuntius horribilis
Ionios fluctus, postquam illuc Arrius isset,
    iam non Ionios esse, sed Hionios.

Hummel and Brodribb, *Lays from Latin Lyres*, 1876

Whenever 'Arry tried to sound
An H, his care was unavailing;
He always spoke of 'orse and 'ound,
And all his kinsfolk had that failing.

Peace to our ears. He went from home;
But tidings came that grieved us bitterly—
That 'Arry, while he stayed at Rome,
Enjoyed his 'oliday in Hitaly.

Carmen 85.

Odi et amo. Quare id faciam fortasse requiris.
Nescio, sed fieri sentio et excrucior.

William Shakespeare (1564-1616)

Cymbeline III, 5, 69ff.

Cloten I love and hate her: for she's fair and royal,
And that she hath all courtly parts more exquisite
Than lady, ladies, woman; from every one
The best she hath, and she, of all compounded,
Outsells them all; I love her therefore: but
Disdaining me and throwing favours on
The low Posthumus slanders so her judgement
That what's else rare is choked; and in that point
I will conclude to hate her, nay, indeed,
To be revenged upon her.

Thomas Carew (c. 1598-1639)

From *To his Mistresse retiring in Affection*

But if my constant love shall faile to move thee,
Then know my reason hates thee, though I love thee.

Carmen 86.

Quintia formosa est multis, mihi candida, longa,
recta est. Haec ego sic singula confiteor,
totum illud "formosa" nego: nam nulla venustas,
nulla in tam magno est corpore mica salis.
Lesbia formosa est, quae cum pulcherrima tota est,
tum omnibus una omnis subripuit Veneres.

WILLIAM SHAKESPEARE (1564-1616)

Tempest III, 1, 39ff.

Ferdinand Full many a lady
I have eyed with best regard, and many a time
The harmony of their tongues hath into bondage
Brought my too diligent ear: for several virtues
Have I liked several women; never any
With so full soul, but some defect in her
Did quarrel with the noblest grace she owed
And put it to the foil: but you, O you,
So perfect and so peerless, are created
Of every creature's best!

Love's Labour's Lost. II, 1, 9ff.

Boyet Be now as prodigal of all dear grace,
As Nature was in making graces dear,
When she did starve the general world beside
And prodigally gave them all to you.

Carmen 87.

Nulla potest mulier tantum se dicere amatam
  vere quantum a me Lesbia amata mea es:
nulla fides ullo fuit umquam in foedere tanta
  quanta in amore tuo ex parte reperta mea est.

JOHN DONNE (1573-1631)

Love's Infiniteness

If yet I have not all thy love,
Deare, I shall never have it all.
I cannot breathe one other sigh, to move,
Nor can intreat one other teare to fall,
And all my treasure, which should purchase thee,
Sighs, teares, and oathes, and letters I have spent.

WALTER SAVAGE LANDOR (1775-1864)

Love's Madness

None could ever say that she,
Lesbia! was so loved by me;
Never, all the world around,
Faith so true as mine was found.
If no longer it endures,
(Would it did!) the fault is yours.
I can never think again
Well of you: I try in vain.
But, be false, do what you will,
Lesbia! I must love you still.

Carmen 92.

Lesbia mi dicit semper male nec tacet umquam
  de me; Lesbia me dispeream nisi amat.
Quo signo? Quia sunt totidem mea; deprecor illam
  assidue, verum dispeream nisi amo.

THOMAS BROWN (1663-1704)

Each Moment of the long-liv'd Day
Lesbia for me does backwards pray,
And rails at me sincerely;
Yet I dare pawn my Life, my Eyes,
My Soul, and all that Mortals prize,
That *Lesbia* loves me dearly.

Why shou'd you thus conclude, you'll say,
Faith 'tis my own beloved way,
And thus I hourly prove her;
Yet let me all those Curses share
That Heav'n can give, or Man can bear,
If I don't strangely love her.

JOHN SHEFFIELD, EARL OF MULGRAVE, (1648-1721)

Song

Come let us now resolve at last
To live and love in quiet;
We'll tie the knot so very fast
That Time shall ne'er untie it.

The truest joys they seldom prove
Who free from quarrels live;
'Tis the most tender part of love
Each other to forgive.

When least I seem concerned, I took
No pleasure, nor no rest;
And when I feign'd an angry look,
Alas! I loved you best.

Own but the same to me, you'll find
How blest will be your fate:
O, to be happy, to be kind,
Sure never is too late.

JONATHAN SWIFT (1667-1745)

Lesbia for ever on me rails
To talk of me she never fails.
Now, hang me, but for all her art,
I find that I have gained her heart.
My proof is this: I plainly see
The case is just the same with me;
I curse her every hour sincerely,
Yet, hang me, but I love her dearly.

ROBERT LLOYD (1733-1764)

Chloe, that dear bewitching prude,
Still calls me saucy, pert, and rude,
    And sometimes almost strikes me;
And yet I swear, I can't tell how,
Spite of the knitting of her brow,
    I'm very sure she likes me.

Ask you me why I fancy thus?
Why, I have call'd her jilt and puss,
    And thought myself above her;
And yet I feel it to my cost,
That when I rail against her most,
    I'm very sure I love her.

Carmen 93.

Nil nimium studeo, Caesar, tibi velle placere
  nec scire utrum sis albus an ater homo.

ALGERNON CHARLES SWINBURNE, *A Century of Roundels*, 1883

To Catullus

My brother, my Valerius, dearest head
Of all whose crowning bay-leaves crown their mother
Rome, in the notes first heard of thine I read
    My brother.

No dust that death or time can strew may smother
Love and the sense of kinship inly bred
From loves and hates at one with one another.

To thee was Caesar's self nor dear nor dread,
Song and the sea were sweeter each than other:
How should I living fear to call thee dead,
    My brother?

Carmen 95.

ZMYRNA mei Cinnae nonam post denique messem
    quam coepta est nonamque edita post hiemem,
milia cum interea quingenta Hortensius uno
. . . .
ZMYRNA cavas Satrachi penitus mittetur ad undas,
    ZMYRNAM cana diu saecula pervoluent.
At Volusi ANNALES Paduam morientur ad ipsam
    et laxas scombris saepe dabunt tunicas.
Parva mei mihi sint cordi monimenta sodalis
    at populus tumido gaudeat Antimacho.

ROBERT HERRICK (1591-1674)

To his Booke

Make haste away, and let one be
A friendly Patron unto thee:
Lest rapt from hence, I see thee lye
Torn for the use of Pasterie:
Or see thy injur'd Leaves serve well,
To make loose Gownes for Mackarell:
Or see the Grocers in a trice,
Make hoods of thee to serve out Spice.

Carmen 96.

Si quidquam mutis gratum acceptumve sepulcris
  accidere a nostro, Calve, dolore potest,
quo desiderio veteres renovamus amores
  atque olim missas flemus amicitias,
certe non tanto mors immatura dolori est
  Quintiliae, quantum gaudet amore tuo.

WILLIAM SHAKESPEARE (1564-1616)

Sonnet XXX

When to the sessions of sweet silent thought
I summon up remembrance of things past,
I sigh the lack of many a thing I sought,
And with old woes new wail my dear time's waste:
Then can I drown an eye, unused to flow,
For precious friends hid in death's dateless night,
And weep afresh love's long since cancell'd woe,
And moan the expense of many a vanish'd sight:
Then can I grieve at grievances foregone,
And heavily from woe to woe tell o'er
The sad account of fore-bemoaned moan,
Which I new pay as if not paid before.
    But if the while I think on thee, dear friend,
    All losses are restored and sorrows end.

ARTHUR SYMONS, *Knave of Hearts*, (1894-1908)

If living sorrows any boon
Unto the silent grave can give,
When sad remembrances revive
Old loves and friendships fugitive,
She sorrows less she died so soon
Than joys your love is still alive.

Carmen 101.

Multas per gentes et multa per aequora vectus
    advenio has miseras, frater, ad inferias,
ut te postremo donarem munere mortis
    et mutam nequiquam adloquerer cinerem,
quandoquidem fortuna mihi tete abstulit ipsum,
    heu miser indigne frater adempte mihi;
nunc tamen interea haec prisco quae more parentum
    tradita sunt tristi munere ad inferias
accipe fraterno multum manantia fletu,
    atque in perpetuum, frater, ave atque vale.

Robert Herrick (1591-1674)

To the reverend shade of his religious Father

That for seven *Lusters* I did never come
To doe the *Rites* to thy Religious Tombe;
That neither haire was cut, or true teares shed
By me, o'r thee, (*as iustments to the dead*)
Forgive, forgive me; since I did not know
Whether thy bones had here their Rest, or no.
But now 'tis known, Behold; behold, I bring
Unto thy Ghost th' Effused Offering:
And look, what Smallage, Night-shade, Cypresse, Yew,
Unto the shades have been, or now are due,
Here I devote; And something more then so;
I come to pay a Debt of Birth I owe.
Thou gav'st me life (but Mortall); For that one
Favour, Ile make full satisfaction;
For my life mortall, Rise from out thy Herse,
And take a life immortall from my Verse.

Alexander Pope (1688-1744)

From *On the Monument of the children of Lord Digby, erected in Sherborne*, 1727

Yet take these tears, Mortality's relief,
And till we share your joys, forgive our grief:
These little rites, a stone, a verse receive;
'Tis all a father, all a friend can give!

Aubrey Beardsley (1872-1898)

(*Savoy*, Nov. 1896)

By ways remote and distant waters sped,
Brother, to thy sad grave-side am I come,
That I may give the last gifts to the dead,
And vainly parley with thine ashes dumb:
Since she who now bestows and now denies
Hath ta'en thee, hapless brother, from mine eyes.

But lo! these gifts, the heirlooms of past years,
Are made sad things to grace thy coffin shell;
Take them, all drenched with a brother's tears,
And, brother, for all time, hail and farewell!

ALFRED TENNYSON (1809-1892)

From *In Memoriam*, LVII.

I hear it now, and o'er and o'er,
  Eternal greetings to the dead;
  And "Ave, Ave, Ave," said,
"Adieu, adieu," for evermore.

ALGERNON CHARLES SWINBURNE (1837-1909)

From *Ave atque Vale; In memory of Charles Baudelaire*

For thee, O now a silent soul, my brother,
  Take at my hands this garland, and farewell.
  Thin is the leaf, and chill the wintry smell,
And chill the solemn earth, a fatal mother,
  With sadder than the Niobean womb,
  And in the hollow of her breasts a tomb.
Content thee, howsoe'er, whose days are done;
  There lies not any troublous thing before,
  Nor sight nor sound to war against thee more,
For whom all winds are quiet as the sun,
  All waters as the shore.

SAMUEL TAYLOR COLERIDGE (1772-1834)

Catullian Hendecasyllables

Hear, my beloved, an old Milesian story!—
High, and embosom'd in congregated laurels,
Glimmer'd a temple upon a breezy headland;
In the dim distance amid the skyey billows
Rose a fair island; the god of flocks had placed it.

From the far shores of the bleak resounding island
Oft by the moonlight a little boat came floating,
Came to the sea-cave beneath the breezy headland,
Where amid myrtles a pathway stole in mazes
Up to the groves of the high embosom'd temple.
There in a thicket of dedicated roses,
Oft did a priestess, as lovely as a vision,
Pouring her soul to the son of Cytherea,
Pray him to hover around the slight canoe-boat,
And with invisible pilotage to guide it
Over the dusk wave, until the nightly sailor
Shivering with ecstasy sank upon her bosom.

TABLE OF CONTENTS